Hanno Scholtz

Civil democracy

Why saving the world starts with changing Greenpeace

Civil democracy:
Why saving the world starts
with changing Greenpeace

ISBN 978-0-244-24393-7

Contents

1	Saving the world	1
2	In a nutshell	7
Part I: How did we get there? A short history of power		13
3	Beginnings	13
4	Europe	25
5	The long 20th century	37
6	Problems of partitioning representation	55
Part II: How to cope		65
7	Civil democracy	65
8	Application variety and strategy	81
9	The adolescence of the world	99
10	Our way	113
Notes		123
References		127

1 Saving the world

Just shortly have to save the world / before I take the flight to you / have to check 148 mails / who knows what happens next / because it happens so much / Just shortly have to save the world / right afterwards I'm back with you...

These song lines by Tim Bendzko (2011, originally German) ironically take up the idea of "saving the world" at a time when the world actually does not seem to be the quiet place it may have been in the past. But is that true? Or are we just imagining it? Is it perhaps an illusion that succumbs every decade or every generation over and over again? My personal answer is clear: Yes, we have a problem. No, we do not just imagine it.

Three steps shall illustrate my point: A look at the global environmental situation, one at the concept of saving the world in public debate, and a brief look at some other problems that concern the world as well.

Probably the most important reason why we currently need to "save the world" is the breathtaking speed with which mankind is currently destroying its natural basis of existence. The most important aspect is global climate destruction. It has changed again and again in the course of history - seven times in the last 650,000 years alone, most recently after the abrupt end of the last ice age about 7,000 years ago. But ice cores from Greenland, Antarctica and tropical mountain glaciers show that the Earth's climate reacts to changes in greenhouse gas levels, and tree rings, ocean sediments, coral reefs and layers of sedimentary rocks show a similar picture: the current warming is about ten times faster than that after the ice age.

Since the late 19th century, the average temperature on Earth has risen by just under one degree (Celsius), mainly due to increased man-made emissions of carbon dioxide and other greenhouse gases (such as methane) into the atmosphere. Most of the warming has occurred in the last 35 years, including the five warmest years on record since 2010. 2016 was not only the warmest year since records began, but eight of the 12 months in that year - from January to September, with the exception of June - showed the highest temperature averages ever for the corresponding months. A large proportion of the heat was absorbed by the oceans, which have warmed by 0.2 degrees (C) since 1969 alone. Images of starving polar bears symbolize the decline of Arctic and Antarctic ice, the extent of which has been reduced by almost 4 percent in recent decades. And on the glaciers in the mountain regions of warmer continents, such as Switzerland, the decline in ice since the mid-20th century is even more evident.

In the entire temperate latitudes, winters are less cold and spring comes earlier. Other weather conditions have also changed: The American hurricane season is becoming ever more intense, in Central Europe the risk of floods and thunderstorms has roughly tripled since 1980, and the proportion of economic output accounted for by damage sums and insurance premiums has increased accordingly. It is also clear that flora and fauna are changing.

And the increase in CO_2 does not only lead to warming, nicely for the climate the oceans absorb a large part of it, but they acidify in the process. This threatens many marine organisms, as lime does not accumulate well in acidic water as shells in mussels and snails, for example. Continued high CO_2

emissions could result by the end of the century in oceanic pH values falling to levels not seen for more than 50 million years. Due to this acidification, pollution and overfishing, life in the oceans is massively threatened. And this does not only apply to water: If humans continue to destroy the biosphere as before, half of the world's higher life forms will be extinct by 2100.↑

And so on and so forth. The world faces massive problems, and it seems that the ability to solve them is not particularly pronounced.

Is it? Isn't it the case that each time has its own problems?

How does the world itself see that? To get an impression of this, we look at the appearance of the concept of "saving the world" in the public discussion, as far as it is kept in books - namely in those books that Google has digitized. On books.google.com/ngrams one may have a look on frequencies of the occurrence of certain words and word combinations over time. What does this look like for "saving the world"? Figure 1 on the next page summarizes this for three language areas: English "save the world" and "saving the world" (subsequently added), German "Welt retten" and Spanish "salvar el mundo".

The values represented in the graph are frequencies per billion words, i.e. per five to eight thousand books: so the values are not too high. After all, they are about five times as high in English as in German and Spanish, as can be seen from the different scales.

They are however not completely ignorable: one billion words are about five to eight thousand books, so in the peak of English values in 1943 the term appears about once per ten new publications - if we assume that in a book that uses one of the terms it appears perhaps five times, then one of fifty English and one of two hundred and fifty German new publications in the years 1943 and 1947 uses the term across all genres of literature and non-fiction books. That is not exactly nothing either.

Figure 1: Frequency of "Saving the world"
in three languages, 1900-2008

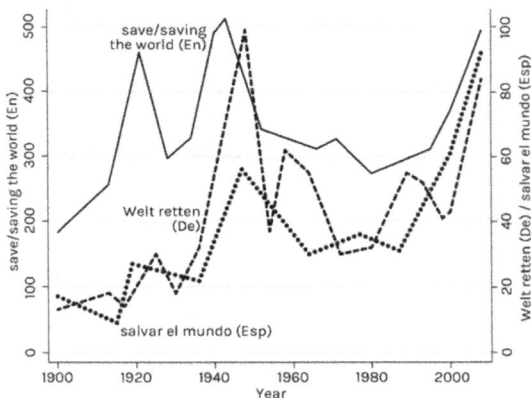

The data show patterns in which the history of the 20th century and the beginning of the 21st century can be read. All three lines start in 1900 at low values, and all three lines between the late 1950s and the early 1990s show a plateau which is not much higher. All three lines culminate in the 20th century around 1945, when the world actually lay in ruins. For the course of values in the English-speaking world, the climax at the end of the First World War is almost as high as that at the end of the Second, while in the German- and Spanish-speaking books the term has apparently found no particular use in and at the end of the First World War.

4

Unfortunately, the dates end in 2008, but at this point they have reached levels that are close to the peak of the Second World War or, in the case of Spanish-language literature, have left it far behind. And with the global financial and economic crisis, which just broke out in this year, and the growing awareness of global environmental destruction, the values are certainly not lower today.

Add to that a few other reasons to worry about the world. The number of refugees in the world has also increased again, and inhuman ideologies have new peaks of popularity, as was the case in the 1930s - later in Chapter 5 we will take a closer look at what parallels there are between the present and these uncertain decades at the beginning of the 20th century.

So there are both a number of reasons for wanting to save the world and a number of people who are worried about it – as much as at the end of the greatest crisis the world has ever seen. Taking the Spanish-speaking world, which was only partially affected by the Second World War, as an indicator of the non-Western part of the world, even to an extent that has actually never existed before.

This widespread awareness is good news. You, dear reader, probably share it. Otherwise you wouldn't be reading these lines.

It's just a question of what to make of it. This booklet takes you through an analysis. *Yes, we can* "save the world" if we take seriously what that means: That we are looking for ways to solve the global environmental and other problems at the same time and to sustainably tackle the increasing instability and dissatisfaction in many nations. In this understanding, the term "saving the world" can be used without irony: it is about preserving the foundations of life in the world in a way that we do not kill each other, but together make the decisions that are necessary both to end climate destruction and to solve so many other problems.

I also believe that we can save the world because the fact that we have brought it to the brink of abyss has one very specific reason. *Our political institutions are based on dividing us into groups, while the opinions and interests of each individual cannot simply be represented by a group.* To understand this reason, one has to go back a long way – the chapter after next starts its analysis with the beginnings of humanity. But when it comes to preventing a possible end of mankind, that may even fit.

And in any case it is worth it. Because the contradiction between institutions that are based on groups and societies that are not is a recipe for disaster that can be stopped. We can turn it off and we have to turn it off. That is how we can save the world. There is no other way.

2   In a nutshell

So one may take the concept of "saving the world" ironically or seriously – in any case, we have to overcome great challenges. This book shows why, and what to do.

First of all: How did we get into that mess? We need an understanding of how things became how they are. Having a problem is having something to do: so it is about the possibilities to shape the world and the decisions that are necessary for doing so. And it is about the "we", hence the structure of human societies in relation to such decisions. Such decisions are never simply private, but they always influence other people. Thus it plays a role who has how much influence there, spoken in relation to the other: how much power. All big current problems of mankind have to do with power. Understanding how we got there hence needs a short history of power. It forms the first part of this book.

And this history of power presents itself in such a way that it is best told in four chapters that unfold in historical sequence. The "Beginnings of Power" (chapter 3) lay down some foundations: man's basic predisposition to freedom and responsibility, the technological distinction between concentrations and more equal distributions of power, the sources of power stemming from physical coercion, from scripture and from differentiation, and the "Axial age" in which institutions were formed everywhere in the Old World to bring the sources of power from physical coercion and from scripture into different equilibria.

Chapter 4 takes a closer look at one of these equilibria, namely the specific form in which power became balanced in Europe. Europe became Europe by developing a very specific structure of society in the early Middle Ages. I call them "groups under roofs": the structure that evolved in Europe divided people into groups and trained them to fit into these groups on the one hand and to accept higher institutions on the other. The innovation in the third century were the higher-level institutions, but what became specific about the European model in international comparison was that it retained groups in the denser and more densely populated continent that remained largely free of overlap. Mathematicians use the term partitioning here, and this aspect is so important in the current problems that I will continue to use this rather technical term in the following. For more than a thousand years, Christianity played a decisive role in partitioning "groups under roofs". And by turning them into organisations and creating competition between them, this became a tremendously successful concept that co-founded Europe's success.

In "The 20th century" (ch. 5) we see how the "groups under roofs" concept emancipated itself from Christianity and, in and after the great modernization crisis of 1914-1945, laid the foundation for the development of those institutions which quite successfully mastered the complexity of the emerging industrial societies. These institutions gave the blueprint for a Eurocentric understanding of modernization that spread sometimes for better, but often for worse, throughout the world. The year 1968 stands symbolically and practically for the fact that finally also in the West itself the society of groups and predetermined positions, with its necessary authoritarian aspects in daily life, was questioned. In between, a half century has passed in which the Western societies became structurally more individualistic, distancing themselves from the partitioning structure of the old Europe and, without noticing it, becoming similar to the rest of the world.

Political institutions, however, are still those that were designed for and fit the partitioning group structure of old Europe. We still vote in elections by assigning ourselves to one and only one partitioning group. And by running or not running for an election, and winning or not winning it, we partition ourselves into either participating or not participating in decision making – while group affiliations and desires to have a say in decisions, have become so diversely distributed for long. If, however, partitioning institutions meet a social structure that is not (or no longer) partitioning, but structurally individualistic, then various "Problems of partitioning representation" arise (ch. 6). We will see how this combination automatically leads to ignorance of issues, to alienation between citizens and politicians, to unfulfilled expectations of representation, to the impression of a democratic deficit, and to polarization – completely independent of participants' individual morale, simply because the institutions do not fit the structure of society.

But we can do better. Institutions are possible to assure stable popular sovereignty for societies without the old European group structure. "Stable" is an important word here – already at the end of the First World War there were extensive experiments with grassroots democratic processes which regularly failed. The reason for this is that they ignore a great deal of half-interest that exists in most decisions: People for whom a decision is not important enough to participate, but who are not indifferent enough that they accept being completely ignored. Representative democracy solved this through group assignments by having all decisions made by group representatives; the semi-interested ordinary citizen had nothing else to do but to assign himself to one of the groups in the election every four years. Nowadays, more people can and want to participate in decision-making, but the problem of half-interest has not disappeared, and the problem of the lack of fit of partitioning group allocations has been added.

The requirement to involve both interested and semi-interested individuals in a suitable manner is met by granting them *meta-decision freedom* – the freedom to decide anew for each upcoming decision whether they are interested enough to wish to actively participate in decision-making, or whether they would prefer to be represented by suitable actors rather than only semi-interested. And the requirement to do better than with a cross on the ballot paper of industrial society can be fulfilled. After all, representation is always representation with regard to decisions. If institutions have the necessary *actor openness*, representation in relation to decisions can be provided by all actors who have evaluations of a subject, who enjoy being trusted with these evaluations, and who are willing to assume responsibility for their evaluations.

This is the first part of the answer to the question posed in the title, why the saving of the world begins with the revolution at Greenpeace: Greenpeace stands for the thousands of interest groups that have a say in the political process. Internally, they all live quite well with the fact that they do not themselves bear responsibility for what becomes of their evaluations. But we are now at the point where civil society organizations must overcome this irresponsibility, as democratic parties did in the 1940s. At that time, they became aware of their responsibility and founded stable party democracy. Today, half a century after 1968, this term has a negative connotation. But it worked for the old European group society and was a huge step forward. Analogously, it is now necessary to establish a civil society democracy, or "Civil democracy" for short. Its derivation and description (ch. 7) will also be a very

10

practical one in part: For unlike in the 1940s, when the technical side of voting could already look back on a long history, the technical implementation of meta-decision freedom and actor openness is something new. Not every in design aspect of civil democratic institutions can however be described in advance, either because they are "constitutional adjustment screws" to be determined in the individual case's political process or simply need further research.

Traditional democratic institutions are based on partitioning representation, and this does not fit for structurally individualistic collectives – they need civil-democratic structures. The tremendous power of this sentence is seen best by filling the abstract description of a civil-democratic system with concrete applications, as done in chapter 8. It spans an arc from small community applications to applications in organizations and the nation-state level in Western and non-Western societies to the level of global decision-making, for example on climate issues. The description of this field provides the basis for the strategic question of where best to start saving the world. Perhaps my answer will surprise one or the other reader.

In the implementation of civil democracy, of course, lessons must also be learnt from the past in order to avoid obstacles along the way. Only after recognizing "The adolescence of the world" (ch. 9) as such, one can deal with it. The European modernization crisis of the early 20th century demonstrated the dangers lurking here. It has led some observers to regard democracy in general as dangerous, but the danger is inexperience: As long as the shaking off of undemocratic institutions and politicians is the project itself, it is not a problem to grant rights to everyone. But when the road becomes rocky, people with little experience of democratic accountability are temptable to take seemingly simple paths and follow elites who propose these. To people who no longer know what democratic responsibility feels like, this applies as well. Civil democracy has to deal with this problem, on the one hand in framing the Civil democratic project as a genuine modernisation project, but at the same time in the form of specific institutions.

The fact that the story of why civil democracy is needed can be described in such a way does not mean that its implementation would be trivial – many people in different life situations will have to work together to bring civil democracy into life and use it to solve the major problems the world is currently facing. "The way" (ch. 10) to this end is by no means easy, but it is feasible. And here lies the second half of the answer to the subtitling question – and at the same time a tiny correction of the thesis put forward. The beginning of saving the world is in fact that individuals recognize the situation as it is and set off on a common path with investing their own resources. But their first demand will be for a revolution at Greenpeace – more generally, that the organizations that have rightly committed themselves to saving the world, or even simply to its improvement in some small aspects, are willing to stand for their evaluations and participate in the democratic struggle for the right decisions in transparent counting processes. Everything else follows.

Part I: How did we get there?
A short history of power

3   Beginnings

All the great problems mankind is currently facing relate to power. In all the great problems we need the power to do the right thing on a large scale, but we also need the insight where the right thing on a small scale has to contribute to the great thing, and with it the responsibility to apply this insight and the freedom to do so. Eight thousand years ago, the relationship between these two, power and insight, came into a state of imbalance that is on the verge of letting humanity prevail to its death. But it has also laid the foundations for bringing this imbalance back into line just in time.

Yet the history of mankind is much longer than these eight thousand years. It goes back at least two hundred thousand years before that: That is about ten thousand generations that have essentially shaped us human beings in the way we are. And in this whole phase of the so-called hunter-gatherer societies, power played a relatively minor role.

Power is the ability to influence someone else by controlling things that are important to the other. At the beginning of human history, we don't need to worry that these things can be different (even if it will play a big role later). First of all you can measure everything together on a scale of "more" or "less". People do things of which they can have more or less: Food, clothes, protection against the weather.

Any "more" had clear limits: The fact that people lived on what the natural environment produced on its own, set narrow limits to the size of groups. This required an ambivalence in the relationship between people and groups: On the one hand, people are accustomed to forming groups. But on the other hand, it has always been an inherent urge to cross group boundaries: Otherwise the small hunter and gatherer tribes would soon have degenerated due to the limited variance of the available genes and would never have learned anything new. Crossing group boundaries is attractive, both in erotic terms and otherwise. Even on a smaller scale it could be worthwhile to cross group boundaries, because other groups often had objects to exchange and so objects that were a matter of fact in one group could become something special in another. But if there were conflicts over resources, in the absence of common symbols and frames of reference, this could also lead to the extreme of genocidal erasure of foreign groups.

Within the small groups of this phase, however, there is only one really important power difference: the difference between parents and children. All other dimensions of inequality were of lesser importance. Wealth was unimportant because there was little to accumulate. Gender difference was relatively unimportant, too, because the limited resources did not make it meaningful to have too many children, so it made no sense to classify people according to their role in reproduction. When we talk about "hunter-gatherer societies", then, certainly with individual exceptions in both directions, hunters were essentially men and gatherers mainly women. But as far as evidence shows, they lived with these abilities quite equal with each other.

But being a kid or an adult made a difference. To be young meant to be vulnerable, inexperienced and dependent and therefore neither free nor responsible. Childhood diseases killed a significant proportion of infants, and there was much to learn. The power of parents over children was essentially a cooperative one, because in the long run only those people could pass on their genetic material whose children successfully grew into this freedom and responsibility. In a world in which life was not easy and in which, like many others, the knowledge of psychological processes could only be kept and increased to a very limited extent, there is little reason to assume that education would have been completely non-violent. But coercion could always play only a limited role; narratives that produced insight were similarly important. For when adulthood was reached, all individuals were expected to grow into freedom and responsibility.

That wasn't just an expectation. The motivation of all human behaviour can be traced back to the fact that for cognitive structures present in the brain confirmation is sought over time, more simply: that goals are followed.↑ As with animals, instinct-bound behaviour can be described in this way: When an animal searches for food, it tries to confirm a certain pattern of saturation inherent in its cognitive structure. It pursues the goal of finding food and eats. This is called homeostasis↑: the goal of maintaining a kind of inner balance. And it is the same in humans, only that we can store and connect cognitive structures to a far greater extent and therefore actively assemble them into far more complex motivations. On a very small scale, we can follow sound events over time while listening to music and generate temporal predictions that generate anticipation↑, and the release of neurotransmitters such as dopamine can also be used physiologically to track how this works (even if the processes are highly complex and far from fully understood). On a large scale, we follow such schemes as goals↑ or projects↑. And this was the case in small prehistorical groups: If the community had to solve a problem, then the solution of this problem became a project which all adults followed together and for which everyone felt responsible.

The fact that power was essentially differentiated by age changed, however, when we began producing grain in the first agricultural revolution. The grain required settlement, it allowed larger settlements and experiments with ore smelting, and finally a first man discovered that with a bronze sword he was able not only to fend off animals, but to exercise power over his fellow men.

This difference is a difference in technology, that is, in the relationship between what you put into an activity and what you get back. Economists pay particular attention to what is the last step in moving from less to more in situations where there is one less and one more. How does the result change in the harvest or the ability to take something away from others with an extra hour of work or an extra hour of military training? And how was that change dependent on how many hours of that kind had already been invested?

This economic view distinguishes two types of technologies. The life of our hunter-gatherer ancestors was marked by the fact that the first hours of each activity were the most productive. You needed more of it, but at some point it didn't make sense to invest more, and that was true of most activities, but certainly of the distribution of production and the ability to exercise physical coercion.

In the Bronze Age, however, the last hour of the investment suddenly brought the most: the farmer who invested his whole life in agriculture was the most successful. And the fighter who invested his whole life in technologies of exercising power. And between them a new equilibrium arose, no longer characterized by equality, but by inequality. For the sword-bearing kings now had more to decide than anyone else. For the majority of sedentary humanity, freedom and responsibility with regard to everything political was over for the time being.

Thus, the Community lost interest as a point of reference: There was nothing more that could be done, others did. In order to stabilize the new situation and to create a different kind of identification with and motivation for the community, there were new stories. They turned kings into gods, and if the resources allowed it, they were carved into stone in large image programs in order to clearly show the fame of the respective rulers and ruling systems, especially the subjects.

The societies were also changed by the new wealth of the agrarian way of life. Some of the wealth they gained still remained with the peasants, and since they otherwise had little control over their environment, their creativity was directed towards having larger families. The controlled rural population grew, and with the consequence that more of the lives of women were spent with pregnancy and infant care, the relationship between the sexes changed.

Much of the other new wealth ended up with the rulers, in the very concrete form of natural things. And since the kings could not simply consume everything, but were also dependent on making provisions for such times in order to survive in bad times, large camps arose. These wanted to be administered, and from this came sign systems with a limited scope of application and finally writing.

In a historically quite short period of time it began everywhere in the communicatively connected eastern hemisphere that the potential of writing to fix stories was recognized. The stories that were told had always had anchor points in what had actually happened; with the possibility of fixing more details in writing, there was now also the possibility of recording more details of what had actually happened, and the difference between the many stories and the one story that had taken place (albeit from different angles) began to emerge.

At that time, only geography set a limit to power. At the edge of the populated country there was always a point at which the efforts to maintain the power of taxation became too high to be worthwhile. For millennia, the populated globe was divided into a growing, strongly hierarchical world of kingdoms and empires where domination made history, and a shrinking world of freedom without history.

To simplify matters, I have just introduced the assumption that everything produced could simply be measured by a common yardstick of "less" to "more". In the dominated world, which produced more than it immediately consumed again, one could now see that this thesis had its clear limits. There were things that were not produced locally, and such things became interesting and important for people. If one had them, one could exercise power over others, partly in small ways by serving them a more tasty meal, partly in large ways by relying on political representation or certain military technologies on goods that were not locally available. Even before grain had been used, things had been traded between groups, and there had even been isolated cases where groups had long remained in a place with special natural resources that only gained value through exchange. But with agriculture, settledness, and domination, trade and a third source of power, diversity, emerged to a much greater extent. Like the power of the word, it is not based on coercion, but on agreement. But in both cases this agreement can be a premature one, in which individuals at a later stage get the impression that they have acted without sufficient information against their own interests, and in both cases it usually takes a lot of thinking and talking to change such things again.

Although trade, the "differentiated" production of different goods on which it is based and the resulting power of diversity are thus similar in age to the power of military domination, it has long played no great role in the visible history of power because the importance of basic things such as food, clothing and housing, which in principle could be covered by local supply, remained so much more important. We will return to the topic.

The more important change for the next millennia was the invention of writing. It was accompanied by the possibility to record stories for many people and to give them connecting clues. This could not remain without consequences for the structures of power and political decision-making. This was followed by a long phase in which attempts were made, in ever new forms, to find institutions that could bring the power of the sword and the new power of the word into a stable relationship. Karl Jaspers called this time "Axial age". All institutional systems that developed during the Axial age had to react to the technological situations on which they were based. And they did so in very different ways, following the differences in the technological situations that either newly created power concentration, hierarchy and subordination or, as in the nomadic period, enabled power equilibrium, freedom and responsibility.

One extreme was China. The geography of a country to be dominated by changing technologies over five millennia each in approximately the same borders created a continuity of power structures from the time of the pre-Axis empires until today, in which only did dynasties change, through technological change or for other reasons, but after each phase of collapse, insecurity and armed conflict followed again and again approximately the same structures of central domination. The written concepts followed this structure and, on the one hand, grasped the behaviours that could best be used in the ramified structures of central rule and, on the other hand, cultivated the serenity that was the most useful reaction for subjects of such a ruling structure to maintain their own coherence and dignity.

The other extreme is Judaism. It emerged in a country that was too harsh for centralized rule and created a situation in which adult society members were able to defend themselves together against external rule and maintain the balance of free people from nomadic times. This ability depended on fixing stories. Israel was close to Egypt, Mesopotamia and later Assyria, the greatest empires of their time. Under this cultural influence, the nomadic tribes who conquered and populated Israel realized that they could use Scripture to unite under a social order and write a history based not on the dichotomy of kings and kinsmen, but on the freedom and responsibility for which they felt created. Despite the fact that Israel, after some time, was ruled by kings as well as other nations around, Israel's leading spirits and the scriptures which they developed and passed on from generation to generation put much effort into making it clear that from God's point of view this was a concession and not a demand. They defined the spiritual goal of a good life independently of politics and sanctioned any political interference in moral behavior. Thus, even under kings or in exile, they were able to preserve as a spiritually important sphere the one in which all individuals met each other on an equal base in freedom and responsibility. In times without state power, the essential institutions of Judaism were thus not lost but further developed and strengthened.

Most institutional systems in between, however, represented a mixture of power concentrations and power balances. A first example is ancient Greece, which today's observer associates even more with freedom and responsibility, namely for the first time institutionalized democratic co-responsibility than with Judaism. In Greece, too, power was not centralised in the Iron Age phase of a relatively general availability of weapons, but widely distributed among the population. In the cities, male adult citizens were capable of military action and lived among themselves in a power equilibrium structure as free, equal and equally politically responsible. Each of them managed to master the important foundations both in productive activity and in that of gaining influence. In addition, the Greek polis was also based on two other foundations: stories mediated between the citizens, which were made up of mixed natural gods and historical events and offered every citizen access to concepts of individual heroism – in which, on the other hand, a hierarchy prevailed, at the top of which each of these citizens stood within his household, and which formed the actual basis of production the longer, the more. The Greek polis lasted as long as the united but individual military effort of these citizens seeing themselves as heroes were at the forefront of military technology. When, around the middle of the fourth century B.C., it began to pay off militarily to lead more centrally into individual soldierly decisions, the polis ended. Alexander the Great built a short-term empire with the fighting power inherited from its tradition, but could not build the institutions to keep it.

Rome, on the other hand, whose rise began at this time, was based on the dichotomy of the two groups of Senate and people. In a sense, it had two levels of power balance of free citizens; the patricians represented in the Senate represented the army leaders analogous to Alexander, the people of Rome the motivated soldiers analogous to the Greek citizens. As in Greece, below them there was the power hierarchy of the unfree, and all this was held together by stories which had been taken over by the Greeks, developed only a little further. But when the empire had become too great, the competition for power among the patricians could no longer be managed within the established institutions, and Rome became a snake pit, in which, as in old hierarchies, there could only be one top and the battle for the imperial crown was fought by all means, until the resulting institutional decay in the fifth century caused them to fall apart like a house of cards. By giving freedom and individual initiative much room, Greek and Roman antiquity were very successful in the Axis phase of the search for an agreement between the power of military coercion and that of the persuasive word; but they did not yet establish that agreement.

Elsewhere, this had happened in parallel and partly much earlier. In India, on the basis of a people invading from the outside a resident population on a geographically diverse subcontinent, a multitude of institutions had developed that largely agreed in that they assigned the sources of power of writing, military coercion and diversity to priests, warriors and merchants as specific groups. The priests were essentially in a balance of power (which before 1600 marked traders in general), and between the warriors everything was possible, phases of balance of local rulers, war and relatively uni-fied dominions, but which never fundamentally changed the basic institutional system of group division and the absence of a religious hierarchy.

But the institutions that shape the world today have been essentially developed in Europe, and therefore it is im-portant to see how the history of power developed here. We take some lessons from this view of the early history of power to the next step: (a) The difference between power concentration and power balance; (b) the difference between the power sources of military coercion, writing and differen-tiation; (c) the importance of both groups and the incentive to cross group boundaries, and the coexistence of exchanges between groups and sometimes genocidal conflict; (d) the fact that balances of power bring freedom and responsibility and that this was the normal state over the ten thousand gen-erations that have genetically shaped humanity; (e) the fact that the populated world has been substantially marked by concentrations of power for eight thousand years; and now (f) the question of how sword and writing were brought into balance at the end of the Axial age in Europe.

4 Europe

When the Roman Empire collapsed, it left Europe as a continent still too fissured for permanent central military rule, but communicatively united by the Roman roads. These roads were made for the power of the sword, but already the late Empire had to realize that in the long run it could not motivate soldiers to travel long distances in order to control people who knew their area much better. Physical coercion technologies of the time were clearly concentrated and the basis for the domination and exploitation of defenceless peasants over one and a half millennia. But this applied locally and never across the continent.

Diocletian, one of the late Roman emperors, therefore experimented with the concept of distributing military power among four "tetrarchs" who administered parts of the empire. But his experiment remained short-lived, because the power of the word remained committed to the traditional Roman hero myths and their responsibility for religion, which, in the absence of an independent conciliation body, drove the tetrarchs back into competition and struggle with each other.

In this situation, Diocletian's second successor Constantine, who as the son of one tetrarch had been in the best position to follow the misery, lifted the spell that Diocletian had persecuted with all his might against the Christians. They had emerged from Judaism as a very small religious group. Christians used the power of the word quite differently: Diocletian's angry rejection had been the reaction to the Christian separation of the power of the word and that of the sword. Diocletian saw the imperial role as guardian of the religious interpretation of the world as important for the preservation of stable institutions, but in fact it had turned from being a part of any solution to being part of the problem.

The new European reality was in fact technologically characterized by the fact that the power of Scripture could suddenly travel faster than that of the sword, and the solution was to separate the two spheres from each other and from the sphere of the people. This detachment had been used by Judaism when it created kings and from then on religion and the community and its state always remained closely connected. It had been further developed by Jews who feared the suicidal struggle of their small ideological concept with the geographically extended coercive power of Rome and tried to prevent it – in vain, as we know. But between the third and seventh centuries CE it became an institutional framework for a multitude of relatively small competing coercive powers within a geographically vast ideological power. Of course, the new separation was not always strictly applied, but it marked a clear difference to the unity of religion and state that had been taken for granted from antiquity to the last pagan Emperor. And after only a short time, monasticism created a social group that drew its social position from serving this ideological power of word and scripture. So, as in India, the group concept was used productively, but unlike in India, uniformity in terms of religion and a clear hierarchy within the emerging church was possible here, and unlike in India, membership in the group of priests was acquireable and very soon no longer heritable. When all was gone from the previous world empire but only the great buildings in Rome which the church used for its own representation, this uniformity in the area of the power of scripture (and its interpretation) represented a common frame of reference which allowed disputes between rivalling military power claims to take place, but nevertheless reserved areas which remained unchallenged.

The new ideological concept was formed by the church fathers. In addition to sphere separation, they developed two other concepts that made it possible to carry out disputes within a defined framework: Trinity, and the emphasis on faith.

The core conception of the institutional framework as a unity of Father, Son and Holy Spirit provided a balance of institutional spheres within the individual self-concept. The pre-modern world transformed inexplicable effects and institutional frameworks into imagined counterparts and personalized them into gods. Institutionalized habits of the ancestors became house gods, kings who had formed societies became king gods, and the various polytheisms referred partly to aspects of reality that demanded different norms and partly to attempts to bring different groups of origin, who brought their own gods and values, into a common narrative framework. Against this, Judaism had invented the unifying concept of a single God who, in order to exclude any attachment to particular individuals, had to remain unimaginable. Islam later adopted a very similar concept.

This path was closed to Christianity: Either it would have led to an identification of specific power bearers with the institutional framework and thus undermined universal validity, or to ideas of equality that were appropriate in Jewish freedom and equality but not in the emerging European situation. Respect for hierarchies and their relativization on a larger scale had to be balanced in the conception of the transcendental Other and represented in its personification. The apostle Paul had already attributed a divine nature to the symbolic figure of Jesus. The reciprocity between God and man, which had been maintained in all ancient societies (including Judaism in the Temple era) through sacrifices, was now replaced by the intellectual and emotional offer of faith in this divine nature. This solution made it possible to have both: On the one hand, a divine personalization for the creation of spheres in which the individual was subordinate, and on the other hand, an equally personalized relationship that relativized this subordination. Like the transformation of the common animal sacrifice into the sacrificial act of prayer behavior in rabbinical Judaism and later in Islam, it served the flexibility demands of a post-axial world.

When, in the second century, the growing interest in Christianity led to efforts to connect it with Greek philosophy, the danger became clear that such dualism could lead not to stabilizing balance but to destructive confrontation. To balance the dangerous tension between the two aspects, the Fathers of the Church promoted a state of mind to a third personalized aspect of God, and the concept of the Trinity was born, stabilizing the pair of regulatory and comforting aspects. Arianism, a first century common sense view on the relationship between God and Jesus, had to and could be banished by the centralized church because it could not establish this important balance. A certainly helpful side effect was that the concept, despite its stability, eluded comprehension and thus contributed to the mysticism that prevented Christians from questioning massive power differences, even when concrete rulers were abundantly incapable.

The application of the group concept had a different productivity besides the definition of nobility and clergy as closed groups, although more important consequences took their time to develop. For the classes of nobility and clergy, it was helpful that each of their members had a local monopoly of power. Subjects should not call on peasant or noble neighbors for help against their rule, members of the congregation should not question the authority of their local clergyman. Just as it was helpful to distinguish between nobility and clergy, it was also helpful to separate groups among the subjects from each other – even if these had no cognitive concept of themselves (not to speak of a cognitive identity). This was helped by the concept of the meaning of faith.

In general, theistic religions construct imaginary counterparts and define what believers can do to fulfill ideas of reciprocity in relation to these counterparts. The religious actions defined in this way are either communicative or behavior-oriented and in many cases both, in different mixing ratios across a broad spectrum. The placement of emphasis in this spectrum shapes personal relations within the religion. Although the relationship is far from perfect, the communicative side is more public and the behavior-oriented side more private. Religious communicative action creates community, religious behaviour can be private. It even tends to, to ensure to the believer and his transcendent others that it is actually done for them and not for human others. In this spectrum, the emerging Christian religion shifted the focus very much to the side of faith, much more than in Judaism or later in Islam, where religious action in the form of individual rituals plays a much higher role. Christianity therefore sets a focus both for the individual and for social communication, in which loyalty and equality of convictions have a high value.

In such an environment, individuals could question others for maintaining connections outside the group and gaining social status at their expense. This mechanism made an individual network without external group relationships as an indication of purity of faith conducive to individual status. In a world where the benefits from intact relationships in the immediate environment were much more important than those from exchanges with distant trading partners, this led to the helpful effect for nobility and clergy of keeping local groups normatively separate. This also included the prohibition of marriages between relatives↑, which reduced the power of supralocal family clans almost everywhere except in southern Italy, which remained influenced by Islam in this respect.

As a result, Europe developed, similar to a greatly enlarged copy of the Greek polis, a world with elites which stood in a certain balance of power (albeit not free of hierarchy, especially in the spiritual sphere) and ruled over groups of individuals who were jointly controlled and who were no longer households but subject territories, which for the start did not necessarily have an understanding of themselves as a whole, and who instead of a full citizen as head of household now had a secular owner of military power and, in addition, each had a spiritual head.

The institutional framework of Christianity made it possible for such hierarchically structured units to exist side by side and in inevitable relationships with each other, with groups that not only existed, but also had clear, normally mutually exclusive membership assignments. Mathematicians call this "partitioning": Apart from occasional exceptions, individuals were expected to belong to one group and one group only.

Based on these preparations, Charlemagne was able to return to the concept of an almost Europe-wide empire, albeit in a model different from that of imperial Rome: the imperial top management now concentrated on its core competencies of conquest and rule-making, while long-term political rule could be left to the independent local nobility, and there was an independent organization for ideological power.

This can be called a "groups under roofs" concept. European society developed in the form of partitioning groups held together by common institutional roofs: Each individual is part of exactly one group, group affiliations are essentially constant, all groups together form society, and are able to accept common institutions and let each other live within the framework of overarching institutions. It was both a structure given objectively in the form of social relations and a culture supported by subjective ideas and norms.

This group-related combination of structure and culture made Europe special. It deviated from the hierarchical Chinese model, it deviated from the locally hierarchical but geographically pluralistic groups of the Indian model, and it also deviated from the parallel emerging Islamic model, which was much more characterized by individual networks that, in a geographical space held together primarily by trade, gave power of differentiation an early prominent place alongside the other two powers. And for a thousand years the European "groups under roofs" concept was so tremendously successful that it still shapes our view of how democracy works today.

First, it has been successful in turning groups within commonly accepted institutions into organisations, competing with each other and harnessing the benefits of organisations. One application of this principle were the "organisations" that formed aristocratic rulers with their subjects. The nobles were in interaction and status competition with each other and could use their territories and populations in that interaction. And when in the late Middle Ages the exploration of nature began which quickly reached the limits of religious dogma, again and again there were noble rulers for whom it seemed worthwhile to protect a resourceful head a little more against the rage of the church, because perhaps something emerged that (such as Galileo's calculation of cannonball trajectories) could be successfully used in the status competition of European aristocracy. Without the "groups under roofs" principle, modern science, which formed the basis of European advancement, would not have emerged.

Another application of this principle were the organizations that merchants created among themselves: From the 16th century onwards, Europeans were able to build larger ships than their Islamic, Indian or Chinese competitors because they could form groups which, through loyalty and commitment, aligned individual action to a common goal. International trade as a further basis for European advancement would not have existed without the "groups under roofs" structure.

A third mechanism was based on the fact that the original group competition between military and ideological power, i.e. in the reality of the European Middle Ages nobility and clergy, also affected the individual situation. Every society knows property rights because it always makes sense to give individuals an incentive to stand up for things by allowing them to decide for themselves afterwards. But the existence of property rights is not a question of yes and no, but can have very different characteristics. On the one hand, property rights are something that opposes expropriation by coercion, and on the other hand they are something that privileges the intangible future over the tangible present and therefore benefits from clear communicative standards. Even if the clergy always had a look at both the very poor and the aristocrats, and so both the social bond and the tax-ability of property as norms were developed as well, nevertheless upholding of the communicated norm of property was a strategy with which priests could use the greater uniformity of the European dogma to gain more prestige among the peasants. Thus, the European group structure led to property rights being stronger than elsewhere, stronger than in China, for example, where coercive power could always benefit in the short term by expropriating subjects, and stronger than in India, where the validity of norms was always geographically limited. For Douglass C. North, who throughout his life has been pushing the question of the reasons for European advancement (and who received the first Nobel Prize in economic history for his work), it was clear that this was a central reason for European advancement.↑

A fourth mechanism lay in the fact that the "groups under roofs" culture, even though it had initially developed to the advantage of local rulers, created islands of liberty in the midst of a world of military coercion that had not existed since Antiquity through its ability to create organizations. The partitioning of society had indeed limited the possibilities of connection across group borders. But as organizations, groups became capable of collective action. And they could do that not only in competition with others, but also in cooperation with another. On this path, the group structure led to the specifically European form of medieval urban freedom, in which at first (with the most famous example of Siena) city districts, but later above all the guilds, organisations of professional groups, determined representatives which in the city council made them collectively capable of acting as a whole and thus enabled the militarily or non-militarily enforced success of self-administration against the

33

aristocratic or clerical rulers. As in ancient Greece, the restoration of freedom and responsibility released forces and creative energies whose results still impress us today.

Thus, in this chapter we have described a condensed model of European history in which Europe develops as a society of groups under common institutional roofs, triggered by the coexistence of mobile and less mobile military power and stabilised by Christianity with its separation of the spiritual and secular spheres, with Trinity and the emphasis on faith. With the mechanisms of organisation formation in the state sphere and overseas trade, the strong position of property rights and European urban freedom, this model explains why European society accumulated new knowledge and productive social practices faster than the non-European world for almost a millennium: According to the economic historian Angus Maddison, the average income in Europe in the year 1000 was about the same as in the rest of the world, and in 1800 it was twice as high. (By the way, for Japan, which was a non-European society that acted as successfully and power-consciously as Europe in the 20th century, a similar model of competition between noble elites under the umbrella of imperial compensation can be observed; but how it worked in detail is beyond my knowledge.)

The real explosion only set in afterwards: Industrial revolution and the imperialist exploitation of the rest of the world only began now, with which this ratio increased from 1:2 to 1:4 in 1900 and to just under 1:6 in 1950. They both would not have been possible without the "groups under roofs" prehistory, and in the institutional change that they brought, the European group model once again played an important role. And as we will see, it is precisely this group orientation that is a problem today in the institutions that have prevailed worldwide under the impression of this impressive success story.

5 The long 20th century

Eric Hobsbawm coined the term "short twentieth century" to describe the fact that this century in Europe was marked by a deep crisis and a subsequent success story in which institutions were fought for and subsequently valid for a limited time. In his view, the twentieth century is bounded by a long nineteenth century that ends only in 1914, and by 1989, when the victory of Western institutions marked the beginning of a new crisis.

But we can also speak of a long twentieth century, in which the specific structure of Europe creates a great difference with the rest of the world, both successful and crisis-ridden, which finally closes again. From this point of view, the long twentieth century is already preparing itself far back in the 19th century and continues into the middle of the 21st century. Right now we are in the process of securing the successes of European advances for the whole world, allowing the gap that has arisen to close again, and trying to limit the ecological cost of the whole process.

If one studies the twentieth century, whether short, calendar or long, a few things stand out: The predominance of the European world (including the USA and Russia), and in it the deep crisis, manifested between 1914 and 1945, but prepared long before, the great success afterwards, and the parallel that since 1989 and increasingly since 2001 and 2016 similar crisis aspects as between 1900 and 1939 show up again.

We have already seen how the difference between the European world and the rest of the world came about, and why it is about to come to an end, but we will discuss it in reverse. Because it is the European institutions that have spread throughout the world, the first thing we need to do is to understand why Europe is experiencing this strange duplication of modernization crises. And, first of all, to see whether we can really speak of a parallel. Is the impression really true that the present is marked by phenomena that remind the observer again unpleasantly of the 1930s?

Unfortunately, there are indeed a number of areas in which this is the case: ↑

- The election of the 45th US President in 2016 has triggered a series of comparisons between the present and the 1930s. Beyond the concept of populism, academic and public discussion is even again discussing the extent to which the concept of fascism, which long seemed reserved for phenomena of the 1930s and 1940s, can be applied to the present.

- Recent migration waves refer to migration around 1900; and in general, globalization since the 1990s shows a parallel to the time before 1913. ↑

- Before the "War on Terror" in Afghanistan in 2001, the First World War already started in 1914 through a terrorist attack. ↑

- The economic crisis starting in 2008 has been often compared with 1929, in contrast to the phase from 1945 to the early 1980s that was largely free of economic crises. ↑

- In the rise of social inequality↑, at least with regard to market incomes, one can certainly think of the "social question" of the 19th century.

- Globalisation also includes the already mentioned fact, with measurable developments leading in opposite direction, but comparable resulting changes: In economic development, despite the two great wars over the first half of the 20th century Europe outpaced the rest of the world with a speed difference comparable only to that with which it is now being caught up again.

There is hence indeed a parallel of problematic and crisis-like aspects of modernization processes. We can speak of modernization crises, twice. As already described in the opening chapter, what we currently perceive as a global crisis is the second of two. And these can be understood very well based on the concepts developed so far. We need, however, two steps: one in which we understand in principle what is happening and a second one in which we understand why it is happening twice and what it has to do with Europe.

Behind the crises is the great growth process in which average incomes in Europe have increased tenfold once since the early Middle Ages into the late 19th century, and tenfold again since then, i.e. by a factor of 100 in one and a half millennia. The rest of the world is, on average, already in the second tenfold increase. At the same time, the available knowledge has increased to a comparable (but unfortunately not equally measurable) extent. And these two changes have significantly changed the structure of how we deal with each other over the last hundred years. There are two mechanisms, the transition from tradition to rationality and the transition from authority to deliberation.

The first of these two mechanisms is about demands for information and whether one needs it at all and bears its costs: In a poor world with few resources and information, once one has found a process as a solution for a result, one sticks to it. "Never change a running system" is particularly true in such societies: once you have managed to coordinate any social process, the creation of social order that you have found has primary importance, simply because it would be too costly to try something else. Tradition is the value that demands to respect this experience and to stick to what one knows. In a rich world with sufficient resources and information, on the other hand, it is possible to try out new things and, if necessary, bear the costs of change: one knows that in principle one can know everything, as Max Weber described it↑, and rationality is the value that demands to engage in such a review and, if necessary, change. Tradition can still be one argument among many, but it is no longer the all-encompassing iron cage without a way out that it has been before.

The second mechanism deals with the supply of information and who contributes it. In a poor world with few resources and information, if decisions have to be made that can be improved by obtaining information, it it useful that the actor who already commands most resources and information obtains the information and makes the decisions immediately. In most cases, this is the actor with the highest social status. Authority is the value that demands that this decision be respected. In a rich world with sufficient resources and information, however, it makes more sense for all actors to gather information and feed it into decision-making. Deliberation is the value that demands that everyone be heard before a decision is made, as Jürgen Habermas has described. This second mechanism also means a redistribution of power based on the power of diversity: a poor, authoritarian society is therefore a society of power concentration, a rich, deliberative one of power equilibrium, because everyone can contribute something else.

40

These two first steps together make it clear that growth and more information will make something fundamentally different that changes life. Without sufficient theory, no-one knows where this is going. That makes people afraid. They discuss different possible ways out, among them perhaps some that do not turn out to be particularly suitable afterwards, and perhaps some try not only to discuss them, but to introduce one or the other by force. These are the hallmarks of crisis.

But this look still shows the same simplified understanding of modernization as the only step that all societies face in the same way as the naive modernization theory of the 1950s imagined - with the effect that afterwards the reputation of any theory of modernization is severely damaged↑, although modernization radically changes the lives of billions of people and it makes sense to understand it. From the last chapter on Europe, however, we can understand why these crises occur twice on this small sub-continent.

The processes of change from tradition to rationality and from authority to deliberation are changes in interactions. And interactions are processes between actors. In other words, if there are groups of people who have found institutions that enable them to act together as actors externally, then these processes also apply to them. Thus, these changes have occurred twice in Europe's history because of its specific group structure, because in Europe there are not only individuals as actors, but also organizations. In the first transition of modernity between the 19th century and 1945, there were only enough resources and information to introduce rationality and deliberation in for the few relatively important interactions that took place between organizations or in the formation of organizations. Within organizations, interaction remained traditional and hierarchical for the time being. The society with modern institutions at the macro level and traditional institutions at the meso level is commonly called industrial society.

For the first time in 1968, starting with the well-educated young people of the richest industrial societies, the available resources and information were sufficient to introduce rationality and deliberation into everyday processes of interaction between individuals. Afterwards, their demands for rationality and deliberation in everyday life have become widely accepted in European societies in the half century since then and found wide acceptance in a large part of the rest of the world since.

With the knowledge of the levels of interaction in society, it is also quite easy to describe the relationship between preparation and crisis. The institutions that allow adaptation to power relations also exist on two levels. Here, the dynamics lie first on the micro-level of the interaction of individuals within organizations, and only later on on the agreements that arise on the macro-level of entire societies.

The distinction between the interactions of people in organisations and of organisations in society as a whole, which is so specific for Europe, thus leads to a four-field matrix of new institutions which have to be found, tried out and introduced. Abstractly they can be described as in Table 5-1.

In the development of European societies, we now have the first three of these waves of institutional innovation passed. The political innovation of the fourth wave is what this whole book is about. The problems of the modernization crises are what caused the two cycles of "saving the world" that we looked at in the first chapter.

But let's first go over what already exists:

Table 5-1: Four waves of institutional innovation (general)

Level of underlying interaction	Level of the regulatory institutions	
	Continuous phase: Establishment of new organisational forms; tension with macro-institutions leads to modernisation crisis	Abrupt phase: Establishment of new institutions at the macro level; solution of the modernisation crisis
First transition: modernization at macro level; interactions in organizations remain traditional	1st wave of institutional innovation: Meso-institutional innovations in the first transition	2nd wave of institutional innovation: Macro-institutional innovations in the first transition
Second transition: Complete establishment of modern interaction, also within organizations	3rd wave of institutional innovation: Meso-institutional innovations in the second transition	4th wave of institutional innovation: Macro-institutional innovations in the second transition

In the field of intimacy and household formation, rationality and deliberation initially took hold in relation to the formation of new households, which, after precursors dating back to the 18th century, were demanded above all in Romantic literature in the second and third decades of the 19th century and subsequently successively adopted. The concept of romantic love meant that young people, especially young women, could choose their partners themselves. But after the wedding bells faded, relationships were traditional and authoritarian, with the power of husbands over their wives, accepted sexuality only within marriage, which was lifelong and understood as heterosexual as a matter of course. In European culture, which had always promoted the autonomy of the household vis-à-vis other relatives by prohibiting marriages of relatives (see above), there were no macro-effects here that would have created a problematic tension.

In the second transition since 1968, the fixed nuclear family concept of industrial society has been replaced by a new diversity of intimate relationships, which makes all questions of the organization of relationship life the subject of rational and deliberative negotiation. Sexuality and the birth of children before marriage are just as much a question of individual decision as divorce and same-sex cohabitation; this even applies to cases in which more than two partners live together, even if these remain empirically rare.

In the economic sphere, the industrial society created the large bureaucratic organization that operated modernly on the market, but remained able to afford traditional and authoritarian structures↑ within markets that were less dynamic and largely characterized by unidirectional growth. Within contemporary companies, rigid rules have been replaced by flexible individual negotiation processes, and the term boundaryless organization characterizes the new permeability of the group border around them. It has become being used for changes that have occurred since 1968 and visibly in the relevant literature since the 1970s.

In the field of qualification acquisition, the industrial society created school education, which provided a fixed educational concept for a professional life understood as an achievement-oriented society at the macro level. Internally, schools remained as pre-modern as the bureaucratic organisation. By contrast, with the end of industrial society in the 1970s, it became standard practice for all young people to undergo tertiary education, not only to learn more, but also because tertiary education is much more individualistic than school education and intended to prepare them to find their own way for a continuous development of their own qualifications in a profoundly individualistic professional life.

In between, there were negative externalities that led to a social crisis in the 1930s. At the start of the emergence of bureaucratic organizations in the late 19th century, the combination of traditionalist expectations of paternalistic care and a liberal ideology of free markets and the resulting renunciation of regulation had unleashed productivity. But as the process progressed, this renunciation increasingly undermined the competitive nature of the economy and gave way to narrow oligopolies or even monopolies. There was no adequate feedback on the destructive effects of this oligopolistic market structure, especially where the economically powerful also gained media power and thus influence on public opinion.

The traditional understanding of school also contributed to this crisis: The qualifications that primary school provided were undifferentiated and about identical for all. As a result, workers were basically productive, but easily interchangeable and without the bargaining power that comes from a diversity of qualifications. A traditionalist self-image of the trade unions also contributed to the problem: Instead of understanding their group-based bargaining power to negotiate better wages and working conditions, they still had in mind the revolution, i.e. they simply wanted to become the leaders in a traditionally hierarchically structured society↑ (as happened in Russia) . Since a large part of the national product was used unstably, depending on economic expectations, and a smaller part went into mass consumption, the resulting high social inequality turned into economic vulnerability and into crisis, expressed particularly in the global economic crisis 1929.

The destructive consequences of ineffective competition legislation, undifferentiated education and inappropriate trade union strategies were corrected in the second wave of institutional innovation, in the USA, Great Britain and Switzerland from the late 1930s onwards (in some aspects even earlier) and in the rest of Western Europe after the end of the Second World War. With the rise of secondary schooling,↑ the differentiation of qualifications began, trade unions found themselves in a non-revolutionary role in negotiation processes and became accepted social partners, and effective competition laws were established. All three developments contributed to an institutional framework of accountability for the long-term consequences of organizational action.

But we are particularly interested in institutional innovations in politics. Here, the European concept of assigning individuals to groups under common institutional roofs had already created a specific institutional system, namely that of territorial states, before the actual modernization of social institutions began. This system makes it necessary to distinguish between the domestic and supranational levels of politics.

At the upper level, defined for Europe by the territorial state, the organizational form with an internal hierarchical structure within a competitive institutional framework is the nation state. After the impulse of the end of equating of state understanding and absolutist hierarchy set by the revolutions in the USA and France, it was introduced from 1820 as the new normality of political organization. From the European elites of Latin America, the concept of the nation state spread (and even in the forerunners France and the USA only really took effect from 1830), until in the 1870s it became the western core of the world system and in the 1970s the blueprint for the entire world.↑ But the old macro-institutions of

diplomatic networks and limited warfare, which had provided feedback on the performance of individual actors in
the traditional setting, were no longer in a position to absorb
the new dynamics of national and nationalist upsurges, and
this contributed to the long crisis from 1914 to 1945. Only
the United Nations, with its balance between the formal
equality of organizations in the General Assembly and many
sub-organizations and the consideration of military strength
in the Security Council and economic strength in the Bretton
Woods organizations, re-established a stable international
system that (despite repeated ineffectiveness in the military
sphere) maintained its internal structure throughout the entire period of stable assignments of individuals to groups.

At the lower level within the state organization, a new
form of organization also emerged in the 19th century: elite
groups and social movements merged into mass parties.
Their mixture of externally modern orientation towards political competition for votes and internal validity of the "iron
law of oligarchy"† is a fine example of the internally pre-
modern structures and externally modern interactions of the
industrial society. But the effort to win votes did not for
every party imply the acceptance of the continuous feedback
by measuring the support of the population in democratic
counting processes. An important part of the social crisis of
the first transition, were two social movements and their respective parties, which in the crisis relied on imperfect modern conceptions. For both, failure in elections was not an ac-
ceptable feedback resulting from suboptimal performance
for voters, but a result of "cultural Western decadence" or
"capitalist delusion" justifying the two's joint rejection of
lasting democratic competition. While the communist combination of modern ideology and hierarchical practice was

able to survive for a long time and only collapsed after several decades of internal inefficiency, the fascist combination of traditional ideology and modern practice fortunately quickly disappeared again from the scene, but after having instigated the authoritarian personalities of the generation to incite half of Europe to ashes and kill millions of people.

The incredible bankruptcy of the leader principle gave way to a general acceptance of democracy as an appropriate form of feedback for parties as responsible organizations, which prevailed in the second part of the first transition of modernity. Churchill's description of democracy as "the worst form of government with the exception of all others" in 1947 drew its prominence from the fact that only a few years earlier democracy had been regarded as a cultural peculiarity of Anglosaxons (and Swiss) and, to everyone's surprise, was suddenly generally accepted as the only appropriate form of political organization for industrial societies.

Since 1968, societies shaped by Europe have not only become more rational and deliberative in everyday life, but with the general end of the binding force of traditions and hierarchies in groups, the boundaries of groups also lost their binding force, as well. Thus the European model of group-based institutions, which spread throughout the world under the impression of Western success, has lost its ground in its homeland. Since then, the European partitioning assignments of individuals to organizations have lost their former monopoly in several respects.

In practical politics, the industrial society assignment of tasks to institutional levels (mostly that of the nation-state) lost its primacy; it was challenged both by the growing importance of supra-national coordination from above and by the demand for subnational legitimation from below.

Normatively, the unquestioned identification with one's own nation-state organisation lost its self-evidence. By 1961, the Eichmann Processes had made clear the limits of the legitimacy of individual action through organisational integration. But in 1968, the fact that nation states as actors made mistakes and had to assume responsibility for these mistakes began to become a broad topic. With the United States and the contemporary Vietnam disaster, and with Germany and the incipient realization of overall social responsibility for the crimes of the Nazi era, this began with two societies with a leading position in the level of development and the visibility of national misconduct. In the following decades, it however spread internationally so that the norm of insight into historical guilt of nation states can now be regarded as generally enforced among the developed societies.↑

At the level of individual actors, on the other hand, the most visible development has been the rise of a new type of organization that has taken on the task of representing all kinds of specialized interests. Their spectrum is broad: it includes the representation of specialized altruistic motives in animal protection and human rights as well as egoistic motives, be it based on being affected by infrastructure projects or throug professional interests. Even the latter, unlike the parties of the 19th century, no longer have the objective of capturing the individual with his or her entire person, but limit themselves to the representation of their specific interests. The great success story in the field of political organizations since 1968 are the lobbying organizations of civil society.

And that brings us to today's problems: Now partitioning institutions meet a society that no longer obtains the old European structure in groups. In the next chapter, we will take a closer look at how this results in political problems, and the solution to which this entire book is dedicated will be presented in the following one. It is however a good preparation to first have a look at what is needed in the area of skills acquisition and wage negotiation – even if the conceptual groundwork here is far from being as advanced as in the field of politics.

The acquisition of qualifications and wage negotiations concern private decisions on individual development. Here, the group orientation of industrial society had made it possible to divide the life course into two separate sections of education and work. The arrangement was based on qualification groups for which there were educational programmes and trade unions. Both stabilised each other: educational programmes created the specific sets of scarce qualifications for which unions could negotiate, and group-based negotiations created the social value of differentiated qualifications that made it worthwhile for teenagers to go through the necessary processes of education. Apart only from career choice, incentives for appropriate decisions were essentially at the level of the group: when unions had successfully negotiated for their members, they benefited in terms of membership, resources and motivation. Schools benefited when the paths they prepared for had the nimbus of success, even though they were more concerned with getting their students to graduation without disciplinary problems. But this remained group-based – trade unions interested in the individual career development of their members (possibly beyond the scope of their own representative competence) remained the exception, as did teachers who felt responsible for their students beyond graduation ceremony.

But individualisation and "boundarylessness" in the third wave of institutional innovation have made qualification profiles more complex. And now there is no institutional structure that would provide support for the new individualized responsibilities. In particular, there are no suitable incentives for actors who would be willing and able to support individuals in making appropriate decisions. The absence of an institutional structure that would respond adequately to the new requirements of efficient individual skills management beyond initial education is central to the current inequality problem.↑

In parallel with the group-based accountability that emerged in the general acceptance of differentiation in training and wage negotiation and spread in the 1940s, we can currently expect and normatively demand that the next two decades will bring forward institutions for individualized accountability. An institutional framework must and will emerge in which actors share the successes and bear the failures with individuals throughout their increasingly confusing lives.

At the macro level, such shared responsibility already exists with the welfare state: The welfare state shares the successes of its citizens by paying taxes and bears their failures in the form of support services, or in the worst case in the form of support for their victims and the costs of prison. In its current industrial form, however, this is a bureaucratic regime in which the small flashes of light of openness are quickly renationalized back into public responsibility: Some municipalities or regions pay for actors who offer career advice. But no one really shares responsibility: it is a sign of professionalism for supporting actors to end contact and relationship with the supported individuals at the end of the cooperation. In spite of the efforts to keep contact with alumni (and thus participate to some extent in their success), this applies even more to the school, which is mainly responsible for bringing individuals onto a good path into life.

Social creativity in Western societies has already produced approaches to solving these problems. Individuals experience support in networks or mentoring relationships (the modern successor to Godparenthood), and both are quite successful.↑ But they are limited in scope, duration and endurance. Many humans do not at all have the chance to have supporting relations, and if they develop, they do not last for long despite the positive effect of relationship duration in general↑, and humans who lose course in life and work often lose supporting networks until finally social work may seize. With enterprise-funded mentoring and career support programmes on the one end and social work on the other, there are formal support processes at the top and bottom of the social spectrum. They are missing in the middle. Here formal institutions would have to be created that consistently provide extrinsic incentives for actors to accompany individuals through their development path. What this could look like, however, must be pursued elsewhere.

What remains is civil democracy as a necessary new institution in the political sphere, which we will examine in more detail in the chapter after next. Together with it we have the term that fills the matrix in Table 5-1. Table 5-2 shows all the entries together:

Table 5-2: Four waves of institutional innovation (specific)

Level of underlying interaction	Level of the regulatory institutions	
	New forms of organisation → Modernisation crisis	New macro-institutions end the crisis
First transition to industrial society	approx. 1820 to 1920: Romantic love; bureaucratic enterprises, primary school, parties approx.	1940 to 1950: acceptance of representative democracy, differentiated secondary education, collective wage negotiation
Second transition away from the industrial society	since about 1968: Diverse intimacy; boundarylessness, tertiary education; multi-level government, historical responsibility, civil society	Still outstanding: civil democracy, responsible individual support

The structure of European society has thus inscribed itself twice into the structure of the long twentieth century, dividing it into four phases of institutional innovation. Between the end of the first crisis and the preparation of the second, there is only a brief period of almost twenty years between 1949 and 1968, in which the industrial society existed with its externally modern but internally still traditional and authoritarian organisations.

And the current problems are largely due to the fact that in current politics the industrial society principle of partitioning representation meets structurally individualistic society. What this means we will look at in the next chapter.

6 Problems of partitioning representation

With very few exceptions, contemporary democratic institutions can only understand what we want if we join one group - this is the way to the technically easiest implementation of democracy, it has worked well in historical Europe, and because of the success of the European model in modern and industrial times, this understanding has set the standard model of democracy that has spread throughout the world.

But in the reality of everyday life we belong to many different groups – this structure has prevailed in European societies since 1968 against the old European group structure, most other societies have always been structured that way, and globalisation has turned the world society into the same structure.

It is helpful to keep the mathematical term of partitioning in mind for the European self-classification in groups, but even without it the current dilemma is clear: *Institutions for groups meet societies of individuals.*

Using group-based representation in societies that are not structured in groups leads to a number of problems. Some of them are well described in a graphical presentation.

A first problem is the *decreasing legitimacy* of political decisions. Suppose there are two result dimensions, a to b and a' to b'. Each individual has his or her own ideas of what is the best, which can be measured independently of each other. Figure 6-1 compares two possible situations. Each individual is expressed by a point inserted at the place corresponding to the two measures of his optimal conceptions.

Figure 6-1: The dissolution of groups in a 2-issue space

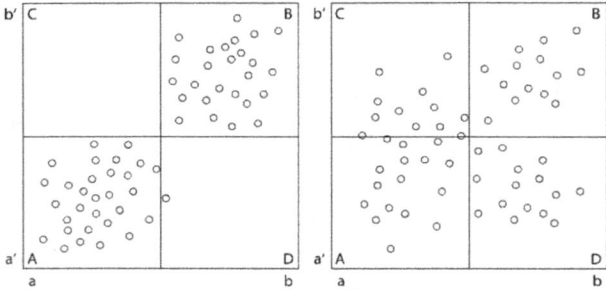

The diagram on the left shows a situation in which the attitudes to the two questions a-b and a'-b' are structured by group affiliations. The two groups A and B each have their own processes of forming opinions, and the individual individual has a certain degree of autonomy from these processes. But it is clear that each individual sees himself quite well represented by his group.

As long as there is such a group-based social structure, two parties PA and PB will serve groups A and B, and almost everyone will be happy: Most voters will feel represented, and if so, they will be able to accept the information their parties communicate to them from the negotiation process.

This is the situation that existed in the old European group-structured industrial society. Severe political debates being found a solution through representative democracy; societies could accept its solutions and go on pacified afterwards. From economic reforms such as the New Deal or the reforms of the French Trente glorieuses to the introduction of nuclear power plants, colour-blind schools, or new divorce or labor rights, industrial societies saw many major political issues that moved their citizens.

These questions were resolved and these decisions accepted because they could be understood as an expression of popular sovereignty. This does not mean that the elites simply did what had been thought up at the regulars' tables. But the regulars' tables, i.e. the locally rooted communication networks that had been constant for a long time, assigned themselves to groups that regarded parties or politicians as their representatives and were able to accept on the whole what they were pretending and negotiating. And on the decision level above the nation state, questions as the renunciations of the German eastern territories, Vietnam and Algeria were achieved, as was the creation of the post-war institutions in Bretton Woods, in negotiations in which each nation brought its own relatively coherent interest.

The development since 1968 can be described in this understanding as in the right picture in Figure 6-1. Voters and citizens of the world have become *structurally individualized*. Not only the radius in which they arrange themselves from group centers has increased, but the group centers themselves have become practically meaningless. In a two-dimensional arrangement, this can still be expressed as groups: large groups C and D have emerged, which no longer feel represented by either of the two parties, or in supranational application by their governments.

In an unchanged party system, these individuals in groups C and D off the main diagonal are not able to express their actual preferences in the voting process. Thus they lose contact with the political process. Without having a trusted representation of their interests, they will no longer be willing to accept the information communicated to them by the

57

parties in the negotiation process. Because they lack the opportunity to bring their own ideas of the world into the process, they become alienated and hostile to a political process and political elites that they no longer represent. Even if they live in a democracy, this *alienation from the political process* leads them to fall back into the self-concept of preindustrial dominated subjects who felt dominated and did not have to control themselves.

This change in the structure of voter interests also leads political actors to *neglect issues* so as not to frighten their supporters: If only the a-b dimension is discussed before an election, the PA party can hope to be elected by C voters in addition to its core A voter group. If PA were to make question a'-b' an issue while PB is silent about it, PA would lose voter group C, while still voters from group D would vote PB due to the fact that there are no "annoying" statements from PB. And vice versa. Each of the two parties has a clear incentive not to be too open in their positions.

One example where these mechanisms have been discussed is the question of the lack of representation of the unemployed by the classic workers' parties PA - they are such a small C-group, for which the question of barriers to entry into the labour market opens up an a'-b'-dimension in which the bourgeois parties PB are more interesting to them, although otherwise they remain more likely to remain clients of the workers' parties on most issues (e.g. benefit levels)↑. Another example is the long-term neglect of environmental issues in international negotiations: In these negotiations, questions in which interests of states as a whole are affected, played a more role than "international public good" questions that affect citizens in each state individually.↑

Social science has dicussed the question of topic neglect apparently only in relation to media: on the margins of the media spectrum, the Internet has produced many new media that address things that they and their recipients find suppressed by elite discourse, and in this area mechanisms may perhaps predominate that do not play between voters and politicians but between readers and viewers on the one hand and media producers on the other. Scientists investigating neglected issues do however point out that the absence of political actors interested in them plays a role.

It is important to mention that the two-dimensionality of the illustration here still implies a simplification. In the 2x2 space of Figure 6-1, even in the new, individualised situation there are "only" four corners of political discourse, and thus potentially meaningful places for self-positioning for four political parties. Nowadays, all party systems based on proportional representation, and even the British for some time, contain four or more relevant parties. This is the natural reaction of partitioning representation to the individualization of the electorate. But there are clear limits to it, because the number of dimensions of questions of content that are no longer clearly linked is far greater than two. With four somewhat independent dimensions, there are already sixteen positions to be filled; if there are ten dimensions, the number rises to over a thousand. No party system and no system of post-election bargaining can provide such a number of parties.

In a third mechanism, an individualized electorate can lead to *polarization*. This may seem odd as first glance, as an individualized electorate is a smaller world and thus should be better able to arrive at consensus. But partitioning institutions are able to shape social discourse to the opposite, as follows: If issues that are not addressed by parties in order not to discourage voters outside their core electorate, such an issue neglect actually makes elections less relevant. It follows that party involvement is also less socially rewarding. In the 1960s, party membership was a source of prestige, but today it is more kind of an embarrassment for which moderate party members feel the need to apologize in their social environment. But efficient party work needs the commitment of members, and as a compensation this leads to the fact that only those who have a particularly pronounced position can be motivated to do so. Consequently parties change from being an image of society to being just circles in which people with pronounced value orientations mutually strengthen each other in their world views. This mechanism seems to play a major role in US politics in particular, on both sides of the political spectrum.

This last mechanism already builds on considerations about motivation mentioned above (p. 20f.): People choose behaviours that allow cognitive structures to be traced over time: they run after bears, they build pyramids, they say prayers, listen to music and pass party programmes. And they receive stories that allow them to think along.

This understanding of motivation makes it possible to solve a puzzle on democracy which a rational, goal-oriented understanding has for a long time had a hard time labying, namely the question of the reasons for civic involvement. In his "Economic Theory of Democracy", Anthony Downs wonders why people vote at all. After all, everyone in a larger community, not to mention national elections, has only a tiny influence on the final outcome, in contrast to small but substantial cost. So, rationally, no one should bother to vote! This paradox is resolved by combining the idea of people following projects and the European group structure: Through the structure and representation of society in groups, voting individuals in industrial society were able to attribute the decisions taken over the course of the subsequent legislature to their own voting action. Through group membership, going to the ballots became part of their own story which gave meaning to their lives. And this is gone.

Forming and pursuing projects, however, does not depend on the assignment of one's own actions, but also on the availability of stories to pursue. And here the general increase in resources and information through the development of modern media technologies has taken on a special form. Media actors live from the fact that their information is consumed less because of its information value than because, like listening to music or playing computer games, it triggers the little dopamine kick that follows from thinking along with a story that can be easily traced. And politics offers many good stories to those who know how to tell them. These are not always the really important stories. But they have their own power. Stories that can be easily traced are characterized by simplification and visualization, by dramatization, personalization and emotionalization, as well as by negativity and confrontation.

Such distortions have to be relativized and one has to consciously search for stories of the opposite side, so that the distortions relativize each other. This is a question of responsibility. But partitioning representation already takes away people's direct responsibility. Now, if they are no longer represented by group affiliations, the indirect responsibility fades of at least being able to attribute a clear voter mandate to one's own electoral action. Many people in many societies have lost this sense of responsibility. They have fallen back into the eight-thousand-year-old childhood of following distorting representations without trying to put them into perspective. Hence, they have become accessible to positions that pretend that the world really is as distorted and simplified as a simple story. In individual cases this may be the case. But normally it is not true.

At the same time, the upsurge in the mediated presentation of politics has added to making partitioning representation obsolete in a much simpler way. Many democracies partition their voters in electoral districts. In the past, most aspects of politics were far away from the perspective of these electoral districts, and after being elected, politicians felt obliged (and did both feel the norm and receive symbolical remuneration) to represent the whole populace at home. Under these circumstances, parliamentary bargaining could be solution-oriented, and finding compromise and communicating it at home was easier.

Mediated presentation of politics has, however, brought everyday's political struggles and the different positions there into voters' everyday life. Hence, voters have a clearer picture of what their politicians are doing. While this is a good thing from the viewpoint of theoretical transparency demands, it has the negative side effect that the voters and party activists who in fact enabled a politician to go to parliament have more chances to prevent non-partisan compromise orientation. The first to acknowledge this new reality very clearly and to urge his colleagues successfully to respond to it was Newt Gingrich. Since his time, directly elected politicians in the United States and to a lesser extent in other democracies have become more polarized in their positions.

A fifth problem of partitioning representation is that they themselves produce simplification beyond the problematic developments of media representation. In an electoral vote, one has to vote on a package that has thousands of aspects in the current complexity of government processes.

For many of these aspects, there are actors who have opinions about them and would be willing to make them available to voters. But partitioning representation would require them to be classified in total packages. Some do, but many don't. And so a large part of the complexity of government processes remains unexplained to the voter. Many processes are also depoliticized technocratically and declared to have no alternative. In a modern world in which the necessity to make decisions and weigh up alternatives is indispensable in everyday life, this is perceived as paradoxical and leads to contradiction and the need to repoliticize such areas and make them accessible to popular action again.

These mechanisms substantiate the first chapter's central proposition that behind all the major problems we are currently facing is the tension between group-based political institutions and societies comprised of individuals who cannot simply be reduced to a group membership.

At the supranational level, the result is that there is virtually no legitimacy, based on individual electoral action, for decisions that have an impact on everyday life. Distorted by business interests, which can often present themselves as the interests of employees and thus voters, they fail in many respects to be environmentally oriented enough, and are in any case insultable as "from above", conceived by elites.

Individualization processes, processes of weakening party democracy, media changes and an unresolved growth of the complexity of governance structures, as we have compiled them, have been named in the relevant literature as central preconditions of the currently rampant populism – and here we have a cause that they all have in common.

Further historical studies are necessary to substantiate the effectiveness of these mechanisms in the case of the significantly lower anchoring and performance of partitioning representation in non-Western societies. Many attempts have been made especially after 1945 to establish modern republics in non-Western societies, but only in Japan with its specific form of the groups-under-roofs concept mentioned above this became a success story. In Islamic and African societies, but to a lesser extent also in Asia and Latin America, these mechanisms have always worked and since the first attempts to establish Western democracy here have led to a situation in which they do not function as well as they did in the West in the 1950s to 1990s. Here even more than in the other cases, definitely more research is needed.

Part II: How to cope

7   Civil democracy

The brief passage through the history of power in the first part has made two things clear:

1. An eight-thousand-year history of power has come to its close. Not that power would disappear completely: But the stable domination of people with military coercive power has ended, and with it, the long phase of forced immaturity and irresponsibility comes to its end, as well.

2. This end is incomplete in two respects. European industrial society was able (following the example of European cities before) to organize the self-empowerment of people through group assignments. But this was incomplete firstly because it was based on a partitioning into groups, which in itself was to a large extent a result of coercion. It hence has disappeared. And, secondly, it left the convention of institutions that have, secondly, lost their efficiency - or did work well, as eurocentric exports to societies without the European structure.

Western populisms (especially, but not exclusively, on the right side of the political spectrum) argue that such a group decision can be restored. All populisms argue with an imagined unity of society and power. But the latter is an illusion and ultimately nothing more than a relapse into traditional concepts of autority that do no longer work in modern societies. And the former would work just as little as the latter and, in addition, destroy socially and economically valuable relationships. Neither is an option for the future and for the solution of the current urgent problems.

Is there another way out?

I think it is. To understand this, we need to take another look at Western democracy, this time at its technology. How did representative democracy work?

What made representative democracy work, and what every democracy needs to function, becomes clear when we compare it with its non-functioning alternative: grassroots democracy.

Normatively, any democracy should be a grassroots democracy in which everyone has a say in every upcoming decision. After all, everyone has the same rights: so everyone should have the same say, right? In principle, this was already inscribed in industrial society institutions. The founding fathers of industrial democracy stated that the highest power or authority "emanates from the people" or "lies with the people, however derived", only that they subsequently established very specific and inflexible forms of "derivation" in which "emanating" was translated into specific decisions.↑

These days there are lots of people who think things should be much easier. Especially in the electro-democratic camp with its well-educated young people, the idea that modern technologies could lead to everyone having a say in everything and everyone could contribute to every decision has many supporters. As we will see, they are in a way right about this – and yet they miss a central point.

In practice, such experiments have usually failed or at least not been transferable to larger contexts. The reason is that we all still have a life and the day only 24 hours. Democracy is important, but it should work just fine so that we can make something of our own lives. And that competes with thinking about all kinds of political choices, about our time and our cognitive resources. For completely rational reasons, we don't all want to think about everything.

Of course, this problem is not something special that would exist in politics only. It is present in many areas of everyday life: If I switch on the light, I don't want to be killed by electric shock, but I still have better things to do than construct my own lamp.

The solution is trust. The lamp on my desk stores my confidence in the lamp shop and lamp manufacturer, that they do not deliberately endanger me, and further that both shop and manufacturer have confidence in the physicists who defined standards for what properties make a lamp safe, and in their own employees and procedures not to sell me a defective lamp.

Trust is also important in politics. In many cases we do not want to deal with certain decisions, or want to deal with them only superficially. Hence, it is good that there are actors, i.e. people or organisations, whom we can trust to make the decisions on our behalf.

This trust is stored in an object again. This time, it is the ballot. Analogous to the fact that, after visiting the lamp shop, I placed the lamp on my desk as a memory of my trust in shop and manufacturer and of the trust I passed on in external and internal standards and procedures, we store our trust in political actors in the ballot paper and make it possible for very specific individuals and organisations to make political decisions on our behalf. The fate of democracy as we know it depends on the ballot paper. The ballot paper is our means to store trust, which is used to decide on policies over the next four years.

However important the possibility of direct participation may be, the institutional core of functioning democratic politics is always stored trust. Because it involves those whom maybe called "semi-interested" individuals: those who do not want to worry about decisions for very rational reasons, but who nevertheless do not want to be ignored in their interests, even if they are prepared to make sacrifices in the definition of these interests.

Unfortunately, this function of storing trust is performed by the ballot paper in a rather cumbersome manner, due to the media technology of paper, pen, ballot box and manual counting.

There is a well-known TED talk by Pia Mancini from 2014↑, in which she describes the situation as follows:

> *We are 21st-century citizens, doing our very best to interact with 19th-century-designed institutions that are based on an information technology of the 15th century.*

Ms. Mancini, like the many other activists debating the future of democracy on TED and elsewhere, did not invest the time to take a closer look at the history of power (and especially its European history) as we did in the first half of this book. That's why they've been unaware of exactly what old technology and old institutions are connected to.

The slowness of technology is responsible for the fact that democracy as we know it relies on two forms of partitioning that worked in the old European model but no longer do so elsewhere and today. On the one hand, traditionally democratic institutions partition into decision-makers and non-decision-makers, and on the other, they partition both non-decision-makers and decision-makers into separate, non-overlapping social groups.

We need to improve the ballot paper on these two points. No more and no less.

The one partitioning of traditional democracy that no longer fits contemporary society is the partitioning into decision-makers and non-decision-makers.

Conventional democratic procedures assign each individual one of two roles from the outset: In the one role, one is involved in the decision-making process. In this case, i.e. the selection of the options finally followed from a range of alternative options available, by comparing them with each other and giving a ranking, perhaps even with the expression of certain intensities, if the difference between two options B and C seems to be much greater than between A and B and between C and D. The delivery of a complete and intensity-weighted ranking order is the maximum that can be done, and for pragmatic reasons one often feeds much less information into the process, even as a co-decider, for example whether one prefers one or the other of two options still available at the end of a pre-selection process. But you have the right to take a closer look at at least two options and make your own decision between them and feed it into a counting process that turns many individual decisions into a collective decision.

In the other role, one is not entitled with these rights. In representative democracy, one is indirectly involved in the decision through one's stored trust, because there are actors who are themselves involved as decision-makers through the trust one has to have in them. But you yourself are out of the game; whether or not you still deal with the decision options does not matter or can only become relevant by affecting the decision-action of one of the individuals to whom the role of decision making is institutionally assigned.

Partitioning deciders and non-deciders *a priori* is unnecessary and wrong. The meta-decision, whether one opts to remain in the half-interested status on an upcoming question or is rather so interested to form an opinion and decide for oneself, is a private decision. It should not be taken away from you, because if you decide in favour of the direct democratic co-decision, then due to this free meta-decision the preoccupation with the upcoming decision and the responsibility for it becomes a part of your own history to a greater extent than if you are forced to it, and of course much more than if you do not have it at all.

Meta-decision freedom combines the stability of representative democracy with the legitimacy and commitment of direct democracy. In this way, it creates a continuity without overburdening the voter, introducing him to accountability. Direct democracy in the form of occasional referenda has attracted criticism for good reasons: Brexit made the problems of the combination of representative democracy in everyday life and direct democracy for prominent individual decisions clearly visible. It is the most prominent example for a direct-democratic decision appearing randomly scattered in a world in which otherwise politicians at the top of party and state structures swaying in the wind of opinion polls decide everything. Such referenda only lead to transforming dissatisfaction into irresponsible protest.↑ Institutionalized direct democracy however that corresponds to the ideal of general individual responsibility however nourishes the responsibility of citizens in decision making. It leads them to becoming conscious of their own responsibility and acting accordingly.↑

The other partitioning of traditional democracy that no longer fits social reality is the partitioning into separate, non-overlapping social groups. It affects decision-makers and non-decision-makers alike, because the common identity as belonging to the same partitioning group that connects decision-makers and non-decision-makers is precisely the basis of the traditional representative model. The European concept of partitioning group allocation in the phase of industrial society has created party democracy and the UN system. But neither party leaders nor nation-state governments can be considered longer the only generally accepted representatives of individuals, because neither party leaders nor governments are joined by homogeneous followers.

The representation of the half-interested, who are happy to avoid the direct confrontation with the comparison of options and are willing to invest trust and perhaps also to accept a certain vagueness in the representation of their interests, must in any case be taken over by actors. These are individuals or organisations (i.e. groups of individuals who can act as a single actor externally through group-internal institutions) who have an outwardly visible profile that makes it possible to roughly predict their future decisions. If such a prediction of expected future decisions of an political actor roughly corresponds to the own interests of half-interested citizen, they should generally be able to let themselves be represented by the actor.

The abolition of partitioning implies that an individual is allowed to simultaneously trust several actors not only in mental affection but in counted representation. Depending on how great the ambiguity is that one is prepared to accept with one's trust, these may even be actors who do not agree on individual questions in every respect. Above all, however, they will be specialized political actors who, unlike parties and governments, do not have an opinion on every issue to feed into the decision-making process.

Such specialised political actors have been around for a long time. We have seen in Chapter 5 that in the field of political organizations the great success story since 1968 has been the actors of civil society: non-governmental lobby organizations or NGOs. Lobby organisations limit themselves to individual subject areas and can therefore adopt much more coherent and trustworthy positions than parties that, in an individualised society, are always offending people with every position they take. While the current crisis of the parties was preparing itself, its successor has been warming up for half a century.

If citizens have the opportunity to spread their trust and in counting processes vote among many actors, it leads to NGOs and, to a lesser extent, politically prominent individuals to being involved in political decision-making. They can then assess options for decisions that they consider relevant to their profile and make these assessments available to the voters trusting them.

In this sense, a new institutional system must allow all kinds of political actors (depending only on respecting game rules) and thus be "open to actors", as opposed to restricting industrial society-partitioning representation to parties. The only relevant distinction is between private actors and open actors (OAs), i.e. actors being private in their decision-making and actors being open in that respect: For normal individuals it is a good and important right to be able to make their decisions privately and without the knowledge of others. This voting secrecy is the only way to allow them to follow their inner convictions, even if they lack the cognitive concepts for argumentative defense for these, or if they might be afraid of negative consequences from others. For trusted actors, on the other hand, it is constitutive to have the cognitive abilities to explain and defend positions taken in order to be able to fulfil the role of acting in accordance with the trust placed in them, but to be transparent as OAs in their action.

Actor openness allows to integrate culturally different forms of trust relationships: With its partitioning of individuals into groups, the representative democracy of industrial society was a Eurocentric concept. Democracy as such is not, it is "the worst form of government except all others" and the natural result of information abundance. It only needs to be open to actors based on culturally specific trust relationships. Trust relations along ethnic or kinship lines are also suitable for representing those who are half interested in a truly modern political system if they meet the requirements of transparency and accepting voting secrecy.

As the sphere of these politically interested organizations is called civil society, and because they and the citizens empowered by meta-decision in their role as latin *cives* or french *citoyens* (in contrast to the *bourgeois* defined by ownership) are the central bearers of such an institutional system, it makes sense to address a form of democracy that integrates these two aspects as a *Civil democracy*.

The basis for being able to replace the two partitions of traditional democracy by Civil democracy with its meta-decision freedom and actor openness lies in the technological possibility of *flexible trust storage*.

So far, an individualized connection between voters, the various decisions to be taken, and the actors to treat them has failed because of the institutionalized separation between voter and election. I call it "vote detachment": Upon throwing the ballot paper into the urn, one withdraws one's hand, thereby breaking the connection between oneself and one's decision made.

In other areas, the creativity of social life has solved the problem of individual allocation in recent decades through electronic storage. This is not yet the case here, due to taboos for fear of violating ballot secrecy. In fact, despite all the progress made in encryption technologies, it may well be that a violation of voting secrecy cannot be ruled out with absolute certainty. But even e-banking and other areas of communication via the Internet that require trust do not work in every individual case, but on the whole they do work very well and are completely suitable for everyday use. On the basis of these experiences, it can be assumed with a clear conscience that the secret of voting can also be guaranteed to an extent sufficient to maintain the freedom of individual decision that is so important for private actors.

A digital storage of trust allocations allows decisions about trust in option-evaluating actors and about the concrete evaluation of possible options in decisions to be continuously fed into a counting system when they are formed: Imagine you see a documentation or read a report about an initiative or another Open Actor and you can directly save it so that it can also be regarded as trustworthy alongside the other Open Actors that you already trust.

Thus, flexible trust storage allows a form of political decision-making in which direct democracy is the central form of political decision-making, but in a meta-decision-free flexible form in which citizens can directly make decisions for all decisions for which they have formed an opinion, but can remain inactive-represented by actors they trust in all decisions for which this is not the case.

74

Figure 7-1 shows the central streams of legitimacy transfer. Their central content is the visualization of meta-decision freedom through the two alternative ways to the counted evaluation as the individual contribution to collective decision: Either as an interested citizen one inputs one's evaluation direct-democratically (arrows 1 in the figure), or as a semi-interested citizen one relies on the evaluations given by the open actors whom one trusts and has deposited this trust in the system (arrows 2-3-4-6). As soon as you have stored trust within the system, this results in indirect ratings for all upcoming decisions for which 'your' Open Actors have given ratings. The moment you have made your own direct-democratic rating, it is valid, even if there is an indirect rating.

Figure 7-1: Civil democracy in a flow model

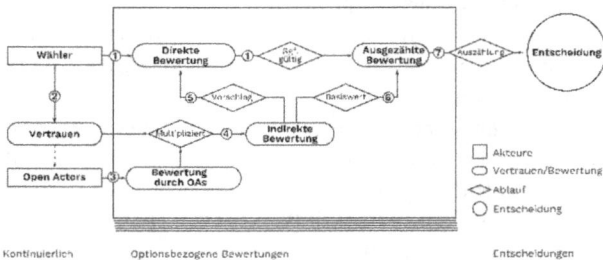

Kontinuierlich   Optionsbezogene Bewertungen   Entscheidungen

An indirect rating serves as a proposal or base value for a direct democratic rating (arrow 5). This aspect has not yet been addressed because it is procedural rather than systematic, but it should not be underestimated: It is much easier to cognitively process a larger number of options for the creation and adoption of a ranking order if these already exist in a proposed ranking order, than to create such a ranking order from scratch – especially since the latter would raise the question of which presentation aspects would possibly influence such a ranking order "from scratch". The Open Actors can be expected to make their rankings well-informed, and no other specification for the individual voter has more justification than the one resulting from the assessments of the individually supported trust actors.

So here we are dealing in three ways (voter–OAs, OAs–options, voter–options) on the one hand with cognitive processes that take place only in the mind or internal discussion of the respective actor, which we call "trust" or "evaluation", and on the other hand with the reflection of these valuation processes in the electronic counting system, for which I have used terms such as "support", "deposit of trust" or "input one's opinion". They connect an active evaluator and a passively evaluated entity. Voters are always actively evaluators and options are always passively evaluated entities, while open actors are in the passive role with regard to the evaluation by the voters and in the active role with regard to their own evaluation of options.

The digitally stored representations of values can be imagined mathematically as sets or vectors of numbers, each of which stands for the support of a passively evaluated (OA–Option) by an active evaluator (Voter–OA). Higher numbers stand for a better evaluation, equal numbers for indifference, and for each active evaluator the sum of the evaluation representations of all passively evaluated persons is one. For the calculation of indirect scores for a decision, the numbers for support of those OAs that have not scored for that decision are set to zero and the remainder is proportionally multiplied so that the sum is one again. Subsequently, for each voter, the vector of these corrected OA ratings is multiplied by the matrix of OA ratings of the upcoming options. In this way, each voter receives an indirect score, which is a weighted average of the scores of all Open Actors supported in the system who have given an opinion on this question. This indirectly generated rating can be changed by the voter at will or of course left as it is before he fixes it as a direct-democratic vote.

There are still many questions for which there is currently no answer or whose answer would go far beyond the format of the representation aimed at here. For one, this concerns the specific procedure: Every digital procedure today is threatened by external interference. There is a wide range of positions on this security threat, from the undisputed application in Estonia to attempts to completely avoid it in the United States. In contrast to conventional voting, in which the ballot paper is entered in the ballot box and separated from the voting person ("vote detachment"), in civil democracy any interference can be recognised and finally corrected by the fact that the allocations of confidence remain bound to the voting persons. However, this is only possible if individuals are willing to disclose their support if necessary. Maintaining the confidentiality of the vote remains a goal, since adequate and action-compliant assessments of decision-making options are easier to enter if the individual does not have to reckon with having to explain himself. But the willingness to pass on trust mandates to impartial persons or mechanisms for identifying and correcting possible disruptions is part of a civil democratic process.

Other aspects are not predetermined by civil democratic principles, but must be regulated separately on a case-by-case basis. I call them *constitutional adjustment screws*. Some of them are very clear and simple, further ahead on the following list things become more complex and technical: You can skip a few things when you first read them and only come back to them when the question actually arises for a process.

- What does the *size of a specific committee* have to be?
- What should be the *size of the minority* that can demand that a decision be taken not in the *representative body* but directly using the civil democratic process?
- Is the vote count for all evaluations jointly supplemented by a *vote count according to specific group assignments*? In Swiss direct democracy, it has had a very stabilizing effect that the validity of a decision at federal level requires not only the "majority of the people" but also the "majority of the cantons", i.e. not only the majority of the entire electorate has voted in favour, but that such a majority is also present in the majority of the cantons. What could such a thing look like for other contexts, and how necessary is it?
- Are voters who are decisive and represented in direct democracy counted equally, i.e. should there be a *reward for direct democratic codecision* and how high should it possibly be? Through the principle of meta-decision freedom, Civil democracy procedurally mediates between direct and representative democracy. The two differ in the weighting of voters who do not make their own decisions: In the representative system there is no other possibility and all count equally, in the direct-democratic system only those who cast a vote count and all others not at all. Through the freedom of meta-decision, it is clear that Civil democracy does not entirely take the side of pure direct democracy. But it doesn't have to take the other side either. It would be quite conceivable that those who take the trouble to look at their indirect evaluation and make it a direct one would also be rated

higher, for example twice or even only with a premium of 25%, because the willingness to participate directly democratically also says something about how much importance one attaches to the question at stake.

- Many electoral systems have centripetal mechanisms that for example favor large parties to stabilize the political system. This is a deviation from a mechanistic form of voter equality and one with a clear normative justification, but the relative weight of the two arguments of voter equality and system stability varies over time. For example, in Germany after 1945 and against the background of the experience of the Weimar Republic, the 5% hurdle to avoid unproductive fragmentation of parliaments was initially regarded as a major achievement, but in recent decades constitutional jurisprudence and changes in electoral law have tended to give greater weight to proportionality in the representation of voter preferences. Comparable centripetal mechanisms are also possible in civil democratic counting. One possible type would count voters' option support in a way that small supports would be relatively more important. Voters who (or initially their open actors) take the trouble to consider more options and distribute their support among them would thus have a stronger role than those who only look at their favorite option.

- With the potential to link decisions, digital storage of trust and hence voting support offers the possibility of tackling an old problem of direct democracy in a new way: Many critics of direct democracy have been afraid of a tyranny of the majority, i.e. of a situation in which same part of the population would impose its majority over and over again in a series of votes. In part, this concern was an artefact of societies structured in groups and has become less likely due to structural individualization. But if this were to happen in reality, the civil-democratic system would make it possible to use the information about who won and who lost in a vote and to give greater weight to the losers of several votes in later decisions, so that the minority would also win in one vote, simply because it has lost so often. This possibility can only be sketched out here and definitely needs further research.

Many of these 'constitutional adjustment screws' are specific to the respective applications, and in some cases (as in the case of centripetal mechanisms in Germany) optimal answers will also change over time.

In sum, Civil democracy is a form of democracy whose central aspects of meta-decision freedom and actor openness, available through using the digital storage of trust assignments, allow democracy in a form that avoids the basis-democratic overburdening and instability and yet makes democratic decision-making flexible and independent of the obsolete old European partitioning requirements – although, however, many specific aspects will have to be clarified in the political process or in further research.

8 Application variety and strategy

Civil democracy as presented in the previous chapter is still just an abstract concept. But this abstracton results not the least from its broad applicability from small communities to the global level.

In order to give more flesh to the bones of abstract representation, the following list describes possible applications. Never forget that at the time of writing, this list is completely imaginative. Out of the list we will have to select one pilot implementation case for civil democracy.

As a small application, one can imagine that Civil democracy could be used by a city or *local government to better relate all activities in a special area of interest to the affected population*, say related to children and teens to the affected families. As births are registered and any child's representation has a clear legal definition, the group of voters is clearly defined in both practical and symbolical terms. Compared with other areas of civil society, there are less representative organisations, mainly because parenthood is always a transitory condition. But parenthood connects, practically all mothers and increasingly many fathers exchange questions with any other parents. They thus form a social network of trust in which political questions relating to children can also be discussed. Who is involved in the planning of the new playground? Where do we need more nursery places? What needs to be done if, after the opening of a new street, more cars suddenly pass by the school? There are individual actors and specialized organizations that would be able to take part in the role of open actors. Many parents will not have an opinion of their own at first, but may learn about their friends and acquaintances through several stages of proposed options and their evaluations. The fact that civil democracy strengthens internal connections and thus strengthens individual parents in their private social embedding is an additional argument. For a city administration thinking about such an application, this argument of strengthening social networking and not least the appreciation of parents and thus voters expressed through using Civil democracy, will play a role in addition to the ability to come to broadly supported solutions.

An application in a church or other *religious congregation* would also be within a quantitatively and geographically comprehensible framework. There are few internal organizations as open actors here: It is certainly rare that church choirs or women's groups as a whole form opinions on decisions pending in the congregation. But every church lives from active members who form opinions on emerging issues and want to be perceived with them. Even in a modern world with more mobility and employment orientation, very classical forms such as communal tea after worship remain important, but it can be very helpful for a congregation, if upcoming questions can be used in a Civil democratic way, to promote connection and exchange between the members.

Even above the local level, civil democracy can be a very helpful tool of the *organisation for value communities*. For majority religions, civil democracy in the context of secularization is not only a possibility for the integration and networking of their members at the local level. Perhaps it is even more important for diaspora communities: The Islamic communities in Europe, for example, have often been accused of being undemocratic, non-transparent or controlled from abroad, or of not facing up to the responsibility resulting from their contact with their members. Especially against the background that the structure of social relations in Islam has always been more individualistic than Christianity (and even, as I argued above, the different form of relationship networks constituted the socially constitutive difference between Islam and Christianity), civil democracy here is the decisive possibility to counter this criticism and to get a responsible formation of will among the European Muslims, which also represents their diversity in an appropriate way.

The ability of Civil democracy to integrate communities of geographically dispersed individuals and to empower responsible collective decision-making is, of course, not limited to religious communities. International migration has led to large *diaspora groups* in many destination countries. These groups currently have their representatives, but their legitimacy is very different and questioned and their ability to integrate the collectives and make them capable of action together is even more different and questioned. Especially in cases with large recent migration flows, the way in which representatives gain legitimacy is slow and inefficient. Individual networking is much faster and can only make its contribution to collective capacity for action with the help of civil democratic organizations. Especially in cases where the primary cause of migration waves is the political situation in the country of origin (as is currently the case in Syria, for example), Civil democracy can lead much more quickly than conventional processes to the formation of capable representatives and to the adoption of jointly-held decisions that can improve the situation of migrants both in exchanges with their new countries of residence and in negotiations with their country of origin. Diaspora communities such as the current Syrian diaspora have networks of trust and representation that exist much longer than the current conflict, and to a large extent the current conflicts are precisely due to the fact that they have never been able to form themselves into a modern and resiliently responsible force as being too individualistic and not group-oriented enough. For these diaspora communities, in view of the fact that refugees bring many differences from home to their destination countries, the consensus orientation of Civil democracy is a particularly important advantage, but the above-mentioned compatibility with non-European trust structures and the guarantee of an impartial counting play an even greater role. Additionally, people who have experienced the feeling of complete powerlessness on their journey will probably appreciateto have the possibility of controling and shaping their own fate as voters. Legitimate representatives contribute on the one hand to the successful integration of refugees into their target societies and on the other hand offer an opportunity for conflict resolution at home.

By organising themselves, such groups become *interest groups* that already exist in large numbers in other contexts. The ability of Civil democracy to contribute to the organisation of interest groups is not limited to the special case (here those of migrants of a certain origin), but is generally applicable. Any interest group that is sufficiently differentiated internally, so that individuals and perhaps even groups are perceivable internally with a certain profile, can use civil democracy for internal decision making to connect its members and these internal actors with each other and involve both more responsibly in decisions. I have already argued that there are NGOs that are quite satisfied staying away from responsibility, and there are also those that only talk about members but mean donors and volunteers (or unpaid staff) only – and such "donation companies" which get along well without internal opinion formation certainly have their right to exist.

But it will be a helpful differentiation to distinguish them from real member organisations for which internal Civil democracy will be a real enrichment.

Parties, the next possible application case, are again only a special form of an interest group, in this case one with a structure that is already designed with the goal of member-based will formation. With their inflexible structure, parties already experience the problems of partitioning representation. Parties are currently organised in territorially different sub-groups, and the fact that the actual conflicts of interest within the parties have always been largely transverse to this territorial organisation has led many parties to have specialised sub-groups for certain groups such as young people, women, workers or entrepreneurs, some of whom also have statutory rights in the decision-making processes. Actual decisions, however, continue to be made essentially by delegates of the territorial sub-organisations and, to a lesser extent, by occasional ballot, with all the problems already mentioned above for partitioning representation and unrelated direct democracy. Civil democracy offers parties the possibility of assigning a greater role to functionally differentiated subgroups that can mobilize more expertise and allow more precise decision-making. It improves the internal visibility of intra-party actors, and competition for them will have an impact on the external visibility of internal actors. At the same time, decisions taken in a transparent and unambiguously legitimate manner after a clearly resolved dispute will result in greater internal solidarity, and by combining the resulting ability to mobilize with the above-mentioned stronger external visibility, the internal application of civil-democratic structures offers clear advantages for the success of democratic parties – even if they thus help to refute the lack of alternatives to party-based partitioning representation at the level of constitutional polities.

Cooperatives are another case of membership-based organizations, with an interest in involving their members and in an open discussion of questions and decisions concerning them. Again, Civil democracy does not work without open actors, so that not every cooperative can be considered – but cooperative banks, for example, which can fall back on diverse networks and internal organizations in which their members are already organized, will also experience civil democratic decision-making as an enrichment of their organizational culture.

Public enterprises are yet another case of organisations with a kind of membership base. They are needed where natural monopolies exist and organisations cannot be regulated by competition. Although digitalization made some natural monopolies obsolete, such as in radio or telecommunications, but others continue to exist. In recent years, public broadcasting in particular has attracted new attention, from one side as newly appreciated place for pluralistic and rational debate in times of fake news, but from the other as target of a criticism that focused on self-reference, lack of internal pluralism and lack of legitimacy. This critique responded to the perceived suppression of unpopular content by developing independent "alternative media" on both sides of the political spectrum. The model of professional self-governance leads to self-referred and elitist media discourse, and external governance is imprecise, biased, or both. The normative assumption that whole populations should perceive their public media as reflecting their views, listening to their thoughts, and being steered by their deeds is currently not met. There is nowhere an independent election of broadcasting councils, so that the control of broadcasting always depends on the same politics it should critically monitor. In this context of publicly owned media., the application of Civil democratic governance would quickly lead to the formation of specialised open actors who would stay out of other policy areas and thus make an independent control of public broadcasting possible.

At the level of state institutions, there is still the possibility of *making proposals* prior to a direct integration of Civil democracy into their decision-making. To the extent that, for example, politicians in economized majority democracies are so busy collecting donations that there is no time left to acquire substantive skills, a creative vacuum has already opened up that is currently occupied primarily by non-transparent lobby organizations. In terms of Civil democracy, this creative vacuum would in principle be filled by the same lobby organisations, but which would now draw both more precise instructions for action and legitimacy from the democratic competition for trust.

An arbitrary example would be the project of better policies for Californian schools, which have so far been unable to keep up with the other successes of the state despite the high knowledge dependency of its most important sectors. It would draw the powerful teachers' unions, which had hitherto only been committed to the internal opinion dynamics of their members, into formalized counting and directly confront them with other actors who also bring in their specialist knowledge. In general, the United States are a rewarding potential application country, with a high current level of dissatisfaction with the political system,↑ and a diverse and vibrant Civil society with thousands of organizations willing and able to evaluate political options. The necessary precondition is, of course, to overcome the current general assumption that blames only individuals or organizational cultures for the current plight and ignores the faults of an institutional system fuelling polarization. A possible example in which the current difference between the productivity of civil society and that of the current institutions is particularly clear would be integration policy. Even for proposal generation alone, in the currently heated atmosphere the consensus orientation of Civil democracy stands out as an argument for it, possibly together with the intensive public discussion of complex issues.

In any case, the interaction between traditional democratic and Civil democratic institutions still remains to be seen, as one example for constitutional adjustment screws. In the long run, it will in most cases lead to a two-chamber decision-making process. The lower the legitimacy of traditional institutions, the greater the scope for Civil-democratic decision-making.

Chapter 4 has argued with a rough division of contemporary societies into the two categories of those mostly Western societies that had a cultural prelude to partitioning but respecting groups that served as the basis for industrial representative democracy, and those that did not. Japan is a non-Western example for the first category, India shows that societies can fall between categories and combine aspects of both. Western societies were successfully organized into groups as the basis of democracy, only individualization changed this, resulting in significantly increased dissatisfaction among citizens. While majority systems have shown greater stability in industrial society, they have recently lost this stability due to their lower integration capacity. The polarizing effect of individualization under partitioning representation, however, has led in all Western societies to policy areas that are not sufficiently addressed. In these areas, calls for joint reflection on proposals for productive policies could lead to joint efforts that could put pressure on established politicians and document the efficiency of Civil democracy.

The scope for civil-democratic decision-making resulting from weakly legitimized traditional institutions is even stronger in societies that did never have an old European groups-under-roofs structure and in which the efficiency of partitioning representation was therefore always not too impressive.

Islamic societies had an enormous disadvantage in the industrial age because they lacked the European mindset of partitioning but respecting groups. Since the 1980s, the importance of individualistic relations of trust in the economy has increased again, and a process of recovery has begun accordingly. But it is still covered by the lack of governance structures that are flexible, information-efficient, robust and non-corrupt, as was industrial democracy in the West. Even in countries with stable regimes oriented more or less towards the rule of law, there are concerns about Islamist influence that could reduce democracy. This development results in part from the same paradoxical dynamics of modernization that made Christian democracy so successful in 1950s Europe: In a society that must build modern norms, organizations that have always addressed norms have a natural weight, and the same chance practicing Catholic Adenauer had got was awarded to Muslim brother Mursi, who missed it for lacking the necessary mind set and the necessary institutional tools. Mursi's authoritarian mind set has, however, been reinforced by the fact that the equation of democracy and partitioning representation actually made traditional democracy unsuitable for trust structures of Islamic societies. Staying with authoritarian institutions could thus be presented as preserving cultural identity. In the course of development towards higher economic and social complexity, however, traditional autocratic structures have become unstable. In order to achieve social sustainability (and ecological sustainability), Islamic societies also need democracy, and an Islamic democracy can only be a Civil democracy.

In most societies of the Islamic region such a development will only be possible against the unwillingness of autocratic regimes. An exception could be the Kurds, the great losers of the territorial partitioning of the early 20th century. For the political actors who came to power among them, the external pressure they face is probably more relevant than the individual advantages they derive from the current institutional structure. Turkey could be another exception: a country where authoritarian structures are currently being further expanded, but where respect (and the demand for this respect among the population) for democratic elections continues to exist. A Civil-democratic-organized opposition that could take up the cause of a stable Islamic modernity applying Civil democracy would have a real chance of success in this situation. Another exception could be Tunisia, the only society in North Africa that managed the transition from the end of the dictatorship in Arab spring to a relatively stable democratic regime. Against the background of the problems of partitioning representation, it is no wonder that secular Tunisians and especially women are concerned about the growing influence of ultra-conservative Islamists. But it is not yet too late to use Civil democracy to preserve the revolutionary gains and balance the polarizing effects of party competition.

To African societies, similar things apply as to the Islamic world. Since many African countries tend to maintain a democratic façade, but their governments then successfully exert pressure on election commissions to support the preservation of established power, the focus of Civil-democratic benefits here is at least as much on impartial counting as on fit with non-partitioning trust structures. A special and potential case of introduction is South Africa. Since the end of Apartheid, the country has tried to do justice to the much larger African tradition while preserving the good parts of its European tradition. Partitioning representation here has so far led to a continuing dominance of the ANC and, as a result, to an erosion of the rule of law and credibility both internally and externally, in which the currently better leadership is not yet in a position to bring about a lasting turnaround. For a government that is honestly interested in good economic and social development in the Rainbow Nation, the application of Civil-democratic decision-making would be a helpful option.

Societies in East Asia have a very mixed relationship to democracy, which is admired for its historical efficiency and freedom of corruption in Western industrial societies, but at the same time questioned because of its lack of consensus orientation. China in particular, with its historical equation of group conflict and chaos, has deeply rooted reasons for rejecting partitioning representation, but not Civil democracy. Despite impressive growth in the past, the inefficiencies of neglecting the theoretical arguments of Condorcet and Habermas are evident in the increasing dependence on individual morality in an institutional system that puts too much power at the top, which could be well distributed, and the consequent need to rely on a security system against which there are no effective fundamental rights. A special case is Hong Kong, which, since its return under Chinese rule, has had to contend with the increasingly firm grip of mainland China. Many Hong Kong citizens want to maintain and even extend their British-style freedoms, while others join the Chinese mainland's scepticism about partitioning representation. In this situation, Civil democracy would be a good solution for maintaining the rule of law without risking population division in a society that has no experience of peacefully arbitrated group conflicts. Civil democracy makes it possible to transfer conflicts into each individual citizen and never partition a single group against the rest of society. In the long term, it alone offers the opportunity to enable Chinese society as a whole to have a governance structure that integrates its citizens, abolishes the corruption tendencies of party rule that are always inherent and always only tied back with great effort, and yet escapes the equation of group conflict and chaos derived from Chinese history.

Finally, the supranational level is characterized by its very own problems with partitioning representation: At the supranational level, group boundaries along which representation is organized regularly run along the territorial borders of nation states. And perhaps even more so than in the case of the dissolution of unambiguous group assignments within individual societies, it is also true here that most conflicts and decision lines no longer run along national borders, but across them. Accordingly, there is a great potential for improving decision processes, decision results and decision implementation offered by Civil democracy in this area.

Supranational does not necessarily have to mean intergovernmental - there are also non-governmental international organisations. Civil democracy, for example, would offer the opportunity for a democratic FIFA in which every person playing football in a club around the world could take part in the decision on the venue and mode of holding the next World Cup. As in other contexts, the accumulation of power among territorially partitioning representatives has led to ongoing corruption problems in the world football association↑. Even if the FIFA representatives are elected by representatives of clubs who are themselves representatives of their club members (which is diminishing in the age of sports commercialisation), the interests in questions of the alternative evaluation of venues, football rules or resource allocation keys are not distributed according to club or country borders. On the other hand, FIFA has a clear demarcation of voters that would serve as a strong incentive. Involving each of the 270 million members of a football club worldwide in the decision-making process would be very much in line with FIFA's occasionally formulated claim to be a pioneer of a fairer, better world in a less politically heated field of leisure.

Supranational, on the other hand, does not necessarily have to mean global: The term introduced for problems of partitioning representation is that of the democratic deficit, and nowhere is this term used more frequently than with reference to the European Union. Laments about a European democratic deficit have been discussed regularly since the 1990s, and throughout these three decades the question has been discussed as to what it is all about, and time and again the debate has been dismissed as a pseudo-problem for an audience spoiled with prosperity. Some of the arguments put forward are to be taken very seriously; after all, the EU has indeed achieved a great deal, continues to allow the member states to take the lead in many areas, has many democratically legitimised veto players in a variety of ways, who accompany every action of the Brussels bureaucracy with objections, and the alternatives to more frequently held referenda would bring new legitimation problems. And yet the debate does not disappear. The chaos that currently accompanies the Brexit process has certainly given the Brussels institutions a certain breathing space with regard to being questioed. But it will come back at the next opportunity, although so far the whole debate suffers from the lack of a valid alternative. There are citizens who demand more participation, but at the same time it is highly plausible to predict that it would always be only a minority who would actually participate. Traditional direct democracy is therefore not an option, but Civil democratic meta-decision freedom would be the solution to this dilemma. On the other hand, it is lamented that there would be no European public sphere, but European interest organisations such as Attac, Greenpeace or the Young European Federalists have existed for a long time, which could establish a common European discussion on the basis of Civil democratic actors openness. Much stronger than the European Parliament that remains too much tied to national discourses and thus has only a symbolical legitimation, but hardly any clear mandate to act, a Civil-democratic representation and decision-making with sufficient participation in the processes of trust storage would be a clear step towards a European understanding of common collective action.

The spectrum of possible applications of Civil democracy culminates at the level of global intergovernmental decision-making with its maximum number of possible participants. Many bodies of the UN system already have consultation conferences with NGOs, but these have no formal, voter-based legitimacy. And this is a problem especially with regard to global externalities, especially climate destruction. The destruction of the climate will only be stopped by discussing and deciding on options very quickly that will intervene in the lives of the world's citizens and that also require a willingness to participate. Saving the world requires more expensive gasoline, dwelling insulation, and flying costs, but more expensive gasoline is hard for rural areas, more dwelling insulation makes housing more expensive, and without cheap tickets, intercultural exchange returns to being a matter for the affluent, so a social consensus on climate preservation must also require solutions for rural dwellers, affordable housing, and intercultural exchange. Here, information must be exchanged on a large scale, simplified by political actors and processed by individuals. There are many proposals on content in this area, but the necessary procedural precondition is the ability of the international community to make legitimate decisions that can only be made by civil democracy.

After this tour de force through the variety of possible applications, the question remains: Where to start? Now that I am writing these lines, nowhere in the world is there an application of civil democratic decision-making. And somewhere you have to show that it works. Where could that be?

In the course of presenting the various applications, I touched on aspects that could play a different role from case to case and help with this decision. It is easier to start with a small number of participants, this argument could speak for a congregation. It is easier to start with people who know that they have a problem rather than with those who are actually quite happy, this argument could speak in favour of approaching Syrian refugees. It is important that potential open actors already exist, this argument could speak for California's school policy or for the global climate. The question of a suitable starting point is thus transformed into the question of the central criterion. What could that be?

To answer this question, it is necessary to bear in mind the complexity of introducing Civil democracy. Applying Civil democracy for the first time requires actors in a number of categories that start simultaneously and in a coordinated way: (i) Potential Open Actors already exist as NGOs, but have internal structures not designed to assume responsibility. (ii) The necessary changes to these structures are not free of charge, so they are only made when the reward is participation in relevant decisions. (iii) In the vast majority of cases, there are always actors for decisions who are legitimately responsible for them, who often have an interest in retaining decision-making power, but who must in any case be convinced and convince their reference groups that civil-democratic decisions are actually better than traditionally generated ones. They need at least one pilot application. (iv) Implementing Civil democracy for such a pilot application has so far been impossible to receive funding because (v) when formulating their application criteria, donors always think in terms of what already exists.

Such mutual dependencies have so far blocked attempts at civil democratic procedures. Everyday language speaks of a vicious circle; social science institutional theory uses the term lock-in. However, social science institutional theory also allows such lock-ins to be investigated. Actually, they are only conventions: Actors find themselves in a situation where it is worthwhile to agree on something – such as a decision-making procedure. One could also agree on a different decision-making procedure, but nobody can start alone with it, a number of actors always have to agree on the new convention. So the right criterion must be one that allows this change from the established to the new convention.

The gap between established conventions with problems and the change to new, problem-solving conventions is closed by social movements. In them, human individuals find a common interpretation of a social situation and build on it a structure that enables them to act in such a way that they get into the position to convince others to jointly initiate the new convention and make it the dominant one. The question of the correct application thus transforms itself into the question of which application is best to start a social movement. Is there any place where the above-mentioned vicious circle can be broken with a social movement?

And I think there is: The one exception to the rule (iii above) according to which the actors responsible for the current decision-making institutions always defend the status quo. While elites in most other contexts identify with existing institutions, openness to change is greater in the global climate discourse. In addition, global awareness of climate problems has created a wide and diverse spectrum of possible open actors. In addition, the costs of the first implementation of a demonstration system are approximately the same for all applications, while at the same time visibility and cost efficiency increase with application size. This means that it really makes sense to start with the largest possible application, namely the global level. Therefore, we start with the pilot case of a Global Sustainability Council (GSC).

9 The adolescence of the world

Before starting to assemble these building blocks into a plan to implement Civil democracy for real decision-making in the world, we have to deal with some dangers of the way.

The modernisation theory of the 1950s was naive in three respects. In three respects, it had deluded itself to a too-simple view of things and thus overlooked aspects that in reality played and continue to play a major role. Only two of these three naive things I have mentioned so far.

It was naïve to ignore the Eurocentric cultural ties of the "modern" institutions that so impressively ensured the functioning of the industrial society of the 1950s, and it was naïve to assume that the end of modernization had already been reached with the industrial society that was still so traditional and hierarchical at the level of individual interaction. These two naiveties (the first of which in other parts of the world had sometimes very violent consequences) have already been discussed. They are the basis of the current problems that we looked at at the beginning of the book.

The third naivety, however, is no less problematic. It consisted in seeing the great modernization crisis between 1914 and 1945 that had just been overcome in the 1950s, and the totalitarianisms of the 20th century as well as the World War and genocide that they led to, as an accident that would play no role in the larger history of modernization. But modernization and crisis were closely linked, and to ignore them naively again would lead to similar dangers.

For people who have not studied the genocides of the 20th century in more detail, the many large-scale atrocities that took place between the genocide of North American natives and the one currently committed against the Rohingya in Myanmar appear to be unfortunate but basically accidental steps backwards to the primitive. Michael Mann sums it up as follows:

Blame the politicians, the sadists, the terrible Serbs (or Croats) or the primitive Hutus (or Tutsis)—for their actions have little to do with us.↑

"Little to do with us" means that we observers, who base our lives on modern institutions, do not have to be alarmed by these cases. The use of better institutions, such as Civil democracy, seems against this backdrop simply as a step forward that makes these regressions less likely.

Such a view would be reassuring, because there is always, especially from the point of view of different religions, also the alternative point of view, which insists that the ability to evil is a universal attribute of humans, no matter how "civilized" they may be.↑ Religion is not wrong with this view of humans either. But the global picture of crime figures shows that there are certainly institutions that have an influence on the realization of this capacity for evil. And in the case of genocides these appear less primitive than clearly modern.

In fact, among the not particularly large group of scientists dealing with the worst cases of genocide and mass murder in Namibia or Armenia, the Nazi "final solution", Stalinism, Mao's Gian Leap Forwards, Cambodia and Rwanda, most have stressed that murder and modernity are linked.

On the one hand, this refers to the "how": besides the availability of weapons, poison gas and highly efficient incinerators, it was modern institutions such as transport and administration that made the efficiency of bureaucratic, impersonal mass killing possible as the Nazis implemented it.↑ And the genocide in Rwanda in 1994, in which no Adolf Eichmann meticulously planned just-in-time delivery to the gas chamber doors, but "primitive" machetes were actually used instead of poison gas, would nevertheless not have been possible without the systematically organized use of modern hate propaganda on the radio↑.

But it also refers to the "why": Modernity and modernization have been held up not only as means, but also as reasons for murder. Max Horkheimer and Theodor Adorno were the first to describe the Holocaust in their "Dialectic of Enlightenment"↑ as the result of a development in which modernity, especially through modern capitalism, leads to an instrumental understanding of man. One of the early specialists in the comparative analysis of genocide, South African lawyer and sociologist (and apartheid opponent) Leo Kuper, identified the modern state's monopoly on sovereignty over a territory that encompasses culturally and economically very different people as a source of the desire to reduce this diversity, to the point of doing so by means of mass murder.↑

The above-quoted Californian sociologist Michael Mann, with the background of having written a monumental four-volume history of power↑, describes ideologically justified mass murder as "the dark side of democracy".↑ His thesis is that democracies tend not to see themselves as pragmatic decision-making institutions, but to attribute to themselves a homogeneity that only works through demarcation and exclusion. In this respect, mass murder is the conse-

quence of an image of society as a juxtaposition of homogeneous groups that can be distinguished from one another,
but which now control themselves anew. In this respect,
Mann is visibly impressed by the fact that the "democratic"
settler societies in the American West (I put "democratic" in
quotation marks because their democratic institutions excluded women, non-whites, and sometimes non-owners at
all) acted much more violently against the Native Americans
than the administrations of the undemocratic European co-
lonial powers.

In this respect, Civil democracy would tend to be on the
safe side. It is based on the approach of overlapping group
affiliations, and it follows directly from this that these groups
cannot be thought of as homogeneous. Moreover, the Civil-
democratic model is aimed at all humans from the outset, so
that even individuals who are excluded from their countries
of residence are represented at a higher level. In this perspective, violence as the "dark side of democracy" appears to be
the dark side of the industrial society's understanding of democracy in particular.

I fear, however, that one does not get out of this discussion quite so easily. There is another approach to how democracy could lead to violence. When institutions change,
people do not change automatically. Everyday experience of
what works and what doesn't, and, as a result, values about
which strategies to resort to, especially in the event of a crisis,
change only to a very limited extent after the end of youth.
Even if some individuals may always learn something new in
detail, value change is essentially an intergenerational project.↑

In the historical case of fascism and the Holocaust, this
is expressed by the fact that in continental Europe the generation born at the turn to the 20th century included to a

large extent "authoritarian personalities"↑ who were inexperienced with freedom and democratic co-responsibility, and who, as a long period of social insecurity and disorientation in 1929 led into the world economic crisis, at least endorsed a violent restoration of the hierarchical stability to which they were accustomed. Against this backdrop, it is not surprising that there were fascist movements throughout Europe↑, even in Britain – although they had very different degrees of success in elections and in the final implementation of their goals.

After the Allied victory in 1945, these movements did not immediately disappear completely, but the failure of their policies was evident. This failure would have come as no surprise for French sociologist Émile Durkheim. The homogeneity forced by fascism contradicted the "organic solidarity" that Durkheim observed in modern societies↑: According to his analysis, modern societies are characterized by the fact that people assume different roles, none of which is self-sufficient anymore, but all of which depend on each other and therefore do no longer get along without each other. Any attempt to exclude people weakens a modern society. This in itself is a robust argument against the use of violence by modern democracies, and in the Second World War it was shown in a radically exaggerated way: After the war was over, Europe lay in ruins and was culturally much poorer than before.

The generation of authoritarian personalities had not yet been able to imagine this. They had fallen for elites who did not have the endurance for the constant social struggle of an open society for better solutions, but rather proposed the seemingly simple way of returning to traditional values, blaming the wrong developments on identifiable population groups, considering the exclusion of these groups as a solution, and on the way also declaring democratic institutions and fundamental rights to be part of the problem. Durkheim would have immediately known that such a scapegoat theory could not work. But the generation of authoritarian personalities was unable to imagine that.

In this view, violence is no longer a dark side of democracy, but a dark side of democratization. Once the experience of democratic co-responsibility has spread among a society, the historical knowledge is passed on that majority decisions must not lead to the abolition of democracy or to the tyranny of the majority: Because every member of the majority is linked to members of the minority, because every member of the majority is dependent on members of the minority, and in a society that is no longer partitioned more and more also because every member of the majority could also be a member of the minority in another decision.

But in a society that still has little experience with democratic co-responsibility and organic solidarity, there are always people who, through unscrupulous or simply short-sighted elites, are seduced into pursuing short-sighted policies of exclusion and supporting those positions as voters or in their respective professional positions (e.g. as judges or journalists).

This argument has been studied intensively by the American political scientist Jack Snyder↑. It led him to a critique of the "export of democracy" of various US governments. With case studies and statistical analyses, Snyder develops his case that in emerging democracies with weak political institutions ethnonationalist violence develops particularly easily, and later with his colleague Edward Mansfield that they are particularly likely to go to war. The argument is the same on both occasions: due to the democratic inexperience of their populations, elites in these countries can mobilize support by conjuring up external threats and resorting to nationalist, exclusionary, or bellicose rhetoric rather than patiently working on solutions. The evidence ranges from revolutionary France to Russia at the time (and today). Since the risk of a state becoming involved in violent conflicts is high until democracy is fully consolidated, Snyder's recommendation follows to postpone political participation and elections somewhat in the process and to focus first of all on modernization aspects such as the rule of law in the external promotion of democracy.

Because such arguments locate the responsibility for problematic developments in societies that are already in a disadvantaged position (for example, because of imperialism or simply because they were not involved in the European innovation dynamics of the second millennium), it is no wonder that the theses of Mansfield and Snyder have met committed criticism. "Who are these belligerent democratizers?"↑ asks a study that examines the thesis with a view to the totality of the countries contained in the comparative democracy datasets. Like many quantitative studies, however, it understands "democratization" as something that takes place in the short period of a few years – Germany is no longer classified here as a country with an incomplete democratic transition for 1914 and not even as a country with weak institutions for 1939, any more than Russia at the beginning of the Chechen war in 1999. With such a narrow demarcation, the thesis can easily be denied.

If, on the other hand, one accepts the disappearance of authoritatively seducible voters with the above-mentioned literature on the change of values only after a generation change, then any statistically reliable predictability disappears in the much larger number of happy cases in which democratically inexperienced societies have not succumbed to fascist elite seductions.

That is good news. But yet, the mechanism remains as a danger. One part of the current crisis are some examples for it. Egypt, for example, elected as its first democratically president Mohammad Mursi, who was supported by the Muslim Brotherhood and who, in his short term in office, clearly showed authoritarian and socially reactionary tendencies and, in comparison with the history of European democratisation, acted more like Hindenburg or Viktor Emanuel, the democracy-sceptical stirrup holders of fascism, than like Adenauer, Schuman or de Gasperi,↑ the convinced democratic Christian Democrats of the European post-war period. And even though it happened against his will, Mursi's historical role was indeed that of the stirrup holder for General al-Sisi, to whom the radicalism of the Muslim Brotherhood provided a welcome reason to largely abolish democracy in Egypt. Another example are current authoritarian governments in Central Europe, which are not suspected of resorting to large-scale violence or even war, but which have not been seriously punished by their voters for severely damaging democratic institutions. Or the election of Jose Bolsonaro in Brazil, whose voters also had no problem with the announced dismantling of democratic rights. Myanmar and India, in which the governments use exactly the homogenization rhetoric described by Michael Mann with in one case threatening and in the other already real consequences of murderous violence against their Muslim population parts, are other current examples.

The seducibility of generations unaccustomed to democracy, on the one hand, to abolish (or at least severely damage) genuine democratic competition and, on the other hand, to violently exclude sections of the population, is therefore a real danger that any policy that seeks the broad inclusion of populations unaccustomed to democracy in democratic decision-making processes must contend with.

In order to understand how to deal with it, it is helpful to look at examples of how societies have dealt with exactly the same problem of low-experience entering into decision-making responsibility since the beginning of human history.

The metaphor of development is often used in questions of the long-term change of societies over time. It has been much criticised because its rise is linked to the naive theory of modernisation and its sometimes violent Eurocentrism. With regard to the ability not to be seduced by propagandists' seemingly simple solutions, one can take the word development more seriously than the "unwrapping" of something "wrapped". This metaphor is a good way of describing the change in societies towards a situation in which each individual has experience of shared political responsibility and acts responsibly in his or her private everyday life on the basis of this experience of responsibility. The citoyen has a different dignity than the subject. The emergence of nation states with elections, which became a farce through partitioning problems, then led under the banner of Western "development" understanding in some parts of the world only to "wrapping" in structures of irresponsibility, and the fact that precisely through problems of partitioning representation, elections have lost their ability to express genuine co-responsibility, has led even in parts of the population of Western societies to a regression, with which the seducibility through politicians damaging institutions and trivializing violence has returned.

The metaphor of development refers to an analogy of acting in the public and private spheres – otherwise we speak of development with regards to the individual and his development from child to adult. There is also a phase in this development in which the ability to make one's own decisions grows without the amount of experience that would be necessary to make these decisions responsibly. The likelihood of making decisions one regrets afterwards, harming others or breaking the law, taking drugs or creating new life without really being ready for it, is never before and never after as high as in this phase of adolescence.

During this time, young people acquire the ability to make free and responsible choices for themselves. But they do not yet have the experience of full responsibility, and depending on the type of education they receive, they may even lack the general experience of making their own decisions and taking responsibility for them. The information they need to make decisions is not yet formed in the necessary way, both in the form of their rational knowledge and, above all, in their intuitive feeling for the right choice (and the rational handling of that feeling).

Mankind has always created institutions to deal with these problems. All cultures have institutions that mark the transition to marriage. But that is rarely all (and only in cultures where young people are firmly under the control of larger kinship structures). Most cultures have additional institutions earlier in life that mark the entry into independent decision-making through a free internalization of norms - examples are the medieval knighthood, religious initiation rites such as communion or confirmation, or modern graduation rituals that support the entry into a life with great individual freedom of choice.

It is worth looking at these rituals with the help of the French ethnologist Arnold van Gennep, who in 1909 divided transitional rites into the phases of separation, liminality and reintegration. The transition from "young" to "adult" involves a change of identity from the former self over a limited period of inner change to return to the community in the new status. This path involves several steps of procedural and cultural acceptance: in one form or another, and sometimes before the actual ritual, the candidates express humility and acknowledge their own incompleteness, the need to grow and learn, and the attachment to procedures - be it in fasting practice before the award or in investing time and energy in learning prior to a Bar Mitzva or in contemporary exams and degrees. They also enter into participation in procedures practically, in any case with the symbolic contribution of their physical presence, in many cases with active contributions such as the presentation of their own research or the presentation of a text. With this procedural participation, and often in explicit commitment, they declare their willingness to enter the community. This goes hand in hand with the acceptance of cultural values as they have evolved in the past, as they express themselves in current self-understanding, and as they are guided by expectations for the future. By naming humility, procedural participation and value acceptance, the analysis of rituals offers a grid that we can use to prevent future violence.

Through the use of Civil democratic procedures, global civil society empowers itself to take responsibility for saving the world. Although, as a group potentially comprising all eight billion earth citizens, it is to a large extent a global society held together by civil democracy and other institutions, it also shares certain values and makes them a community in the search for a common solution to global problems.

At present, these are the values of Civil-democratic co-operation: firstly, respect for others and their acceptance as people with their own experience; secondly, a commitment to keeping the secret of voting; and thirdly, a willingness to support and protect the institutions of joint decision-making.

All these aspects are not self-evident. Respect and acceptance affect parts of world society that are currently in confrontation and do not see themselves as part of a global community with a common history with the common goal of making common sustainability possible. The commitment to Civil-democratic institutions places them higher than other value systems and puts these into perspective. The preservation of the secret of voting stands between the two and is therefore threatened from both sides and must be defended in both directions, both from a non-acceptance of the other as the source of a position worth protecting in their privacy and from a non-acceptance of the common institutions.

The view of the global past is marked by division and different cultures with different achievements and problems. Everyone who enters the global community from one of these different cultures continues to bear responsibility for their own traditions and in particular for their problematic aspects. These do not disappear if you negate them, but only if you actively break away from them. Entering the community means concentrating on one's own responsibilities from a divided past: This social learning process, which developed very slowly in Europe after 1945 and more rapidly after 1985, is a necessity without whose acceptance shared responsibility cannot be sustainable. Finally and above all, the global future is shaped by the need to cope with the finite nature of resources and environmental problems, which is why all cultural traditions based on the idea that the earth is a vast and endless area waiting to be conquered and filled by population growth must be called into question.

Commitments to values, however, remain to a certain extent toothless if violations against them are not sanctioned. For a future in which Civil-democratic procedures for real political decision-making are implemented in society, legal sanctions need also be considered. From the outset, however, institutional precautions can and must also be taken within the Civil democratic system. However, these should primarily be directed against such policies and elites that oppose the values of respect, vote secrecy and institutional safeguarding. The starting point for this is the international interdependence that is possible and necessary for a Civil democratic system. Both for reasons of technical realization and (and much more) for the sake of organizational networking, a Civil democratic system is necessarily an international system on the one hand, and a uniform system on the other.

This makes it possible to exclude actors and options. Such an exclusion must of course have a legal form, and the decision on it must be taken by judges who are appointed for this purpose and who are independent of political influence. In order to prevent the preparation of non-sustainable policies by the appropriate composition of the judiciary, the world population is not represented in its election with the same vote for each person, but according to individual experiences of responsible participation in public decision making. Young people and those from societies who still have little or no experience of democratic self-responsibility must be patient here - to an extent that must be determined in detail on the basis of a follow-up to the above-mentioned research. Individuals from societies without democratic experience thus enter into a process in which their full sovereignty only extends over time, but always lies in a historical perspective. This latter aspect is probably the most important manifestation of the aspect of humility that is necessary for entry into a civil democratic process and thus into democratic co-responsibility at all levels.

These values, respect for the other, keeping voting secrecy, defending the institutions, responsibility for one's own traditions, respect for the finiteness of resources and humility in entering, must be expressed in a declaration of commitment to be made by each voter at the beginning of civil democratic participation. Nowadays, this is quickly done with an approving mouse click to continue to next page. But it is worth remembering to use more ritualized procedures.

10 Our way

Dear reader, no matter if you have read the book from page 1 or if you have followed a suggestion to open it directly here: Now you want to know how you can save the world.

If you have read this far, you will already know the Whys, the Civil-democratic procedure and terms like Open Actors. Otherwise you don't. Helping with understanding the reasons is more convincing for most people, but you can also do the reading later – and as a quick, help I have inserted page references in the following. Now to your question:

What can you do now, here and now?

Step 1: Connect yourself

The first step is to get in touch with the Civil democratic movement. Nowadays connecting starts on the internet, with a Like on Facebook, an email or, if you like, already an entry on our website↑ – which I'll discuss below. On the web you can see how far we we have come so far and which steps are the necessary ones at the moment. Now at the time of writing there is almost nothing. But this will change in the next time, first slowly and faster and faster afterwards. So what you are reading now is written from this perspective of the very start – when you come to it later, you may find that some steps have already been taken. In that case just read on; you will find your point where you can participate in real life. What you can do quite soon is to make others aware of the Civil democratic movement, both online and offline, with sharing our entries on social networks on the one hand and by sharing this book with friends and colleagues on the other hand.

Another part of this process is to become a member of the Global Sustainability Council Association, the organization that starts and runs the Global Sustainability Council, the first civil democratic application.

The Global Sustainability Council (GSC) is a body which itself is elected using the civil democracy procedure and which prepares decisions on sustainability issues for the attention of the world's population using civil democracy. After its initial election it will not yet have any authority whatsoever. But that will change quickly: As a democratic voice of the world population and an efficient place for making decisions on global issues, it will fill a large gap and serve as an example for other civil democracy applications.

Step 2: Help us to find candidates

We are currently looking for candidates for the GSC. People who are willing to run for it must be willing to enter the civil democratic process. As GSC candidates and GSC members, they will be in close contact and exchange with NGOs and other Open Actors about what decisions are pending and what options already exist, and they will receive new proposals for decisions and options for decisions from the Open Actors. The GSC constitutes itself and has the legitimacy to make many decisions itself. But its most important rule is that at any time a qualified minority of its members or the Open Actors supporting them can cause a decision to be made in the civil democratic process, so that ultimately the participating world population can directly make the decision on this issue.

In search for candidates we will start asking some members of the International Panel on Climate Change (IPCC). Most of them are professors of meteorology. We approach them being aware that their role will partly be one of transition: Academics argue on the basis of their special knowledge. They are used to making their expertise understandable to others, but they rarely see themselves as group representatives. At the same time, they have by far the longest lead in pointing out issues of global sustainability, and some of them have already gained some experience in the political process.

After these professors, we will turn to activists and publicists working on global sustainability issues, combining expertise and networking with a variety of stakeholders. The aim is to get a list of people here who are ready to really run for office – that is, to go through a competitive selection process in which others may end up being chosen and not them. Saving the world should be worth to leave behind one's own vanity.

Step 3: Help us to convince NGOs

When we have such an initial list of candidates, the real revolution begins. Those political actors who have the knowledge, reputation and public trust to choose between them as options are the actors of global civil society, NGOs like Greenpeace, the WWF, Friends of the Earth and many others. Some, or perhaps all, of the candidates will also directly solicit voter support. But a profile that combines knowledge, awareness and trust must be built with energy over time, and people always have limited resources available, while organisations like Greenpeace can bundle the energy of many people over a long period of time and bring them together in a tradition.

Yet it is a revolution to address them: NGOs have accumulated some experience of participating in political decisions. But it will be a completely new experience for them to stand for this in a transparent electoral process. Their organizations will have to change internally if they are to compete not only for resources of active and financial support, but also for the support of voters, and if at least this support from voters (and in the long run probably also the financial support) is transparent to the outside world. For many of them, it is not too much of a change, but it is definitely a change for them. But here lies the statement of the book title: *As long as organizations such as Greenpeace are adamant about assuming this responsibility, the world will not be saved.*

You can look at the candidates yourself and consider which of them you would like to support, and to what extent, in order to be an open actor yourself by revealing these assessments. Maybe you will join forces with others. It is certainly helpful if you give yourself a distinguishable profile that will enable you to evaluate options for upcoming decisions in the future and thus participate in them.

But then, perhaps triggered by the example of your appearance as an Open Actor, there will also be the first existing NGOs that can get involved. Some civil society actor will find it exciting to be the first to support certain candidates and later certain decisions as the mouthpiece of a global electorate. And when the first NGOs get involved, others will follow suit.

Step 4: Help us with funding

Until then, however, the civil-democratic model only exists as an idea.

It is hence a real challenge for your imagination. How exactly is it possible for voters to give their support to Open Actors? And how can these evaluate options and let voters understand what has been done with their support? I have answered these and other questions in the fifth chapter of this book, up to pictures of what it would look like on your mobile. But this is still hypothetical. We need the opportunity to experience it. That is, we need money.

Maybe you're in the lucky position of helping us here with a larger amount, maybe even one that already makes it possible to start with a prototype. Maybe you are only able to help with a very small contribution. But in any case you can, and civil society actors who participate in the GSC as Open Actors can, spread a call for crowd-funding.

Until we start this crowdfunding, we need more to describe the civil democratic model than this book and the texts↑ I have written in recent years. We need a better website. We need a video. Can you put idea and concept in three minutes? I think so, but I can't do it myself. See if, at the time that you're reading this, such a video already exists, and if you find the existing website convincing. And if not, and if you are familiar with videos or websites, helping in this area would be a great way to support us.

Such crowdfunding will perhaps bring enough money directly to enable coding a civil democratic platform. In any case, it will open the door to raising money from foundations. One of the negative aspects of the current world situation is that there are many very rich people. But at least this has the advantage that some of them have recognized the seriousness of the situation and are willing to give something back to society from their privileged position and establish foundations. Such foundations have the problem of always being confronted with a very large number of projects, all of which may be worth supporting. That is why foundations use limitations and fixed schemes, and that is why it is difficult for really new ideas as civil democracy, i.e. ideas which do not fit to pre-existing schemes, to be considered by foundations at all.

Many foundations however are willing to give a try to projects that have already been able to set up a crowdfunding campaign. In that case, their boards of trustees do not have to bear the responsibility of judging the project on their own. You have already relieved them of this responsibility, in a small part.

Step 5: Help us to realize the project

With the money raised we can start coding the core of a civil democratic trust storage and decision-making system.

I deliberately say "the core", as civil democracy will soon need offline interfaces as well, since for good reasons many people do not want to entrust such private decisions as trust in civil society actors to the internet, or because in some societies the norm is not sufficiently observed that nobody should be persuaded to disclose what he or she enters on his or her mobile phone in terms of trust transfer or option ranking. These are challenges that we, as a civil-democratic movement, must see and address. But not at the very beginning.

An essential core of civil democratic trust storage and decision-making will always be internet-based and will work using the mobile phone as interface. At least among the more educated and younger people in wealthy societies there are enough who are able to defend the privacy of their decisions and not be deterred by entering of what they really think – not even by the unlikely but existing possibility that their data could be hacked. For those who don't have that assurance, we will find other, more secure ways to enter. But to demonstrate what civil democracy can do to save the world, it is enough to start with this core group.

For them, and hopefully also for you, we will program a civil society platform with the money raised. In order to make sure that when counting the votes no one writes some code snippet that unfairly favors certain options, the entire civil democratic process will have to be pursued as an open source project. And this means that other programmers can also participate than those we will hire to write code in the beginning. In fact, open source projects have their own dynamics, which I'm almost completely unfamiliar with now that I'm writing this. But maybe you are? Support in this area would also be very helpful.

Once this platform is programmed, it starts with presenting, negotiating, and making decisions for the Global Sustainability Council. The first decision to be made will be about the first composition of the GSC. Which of the candidates will be mandated to be the first GSC to represent the world's population? This will immediately be followed by the first decision on the matter, namely on agenda-setting and procedure. How will the GSC work at the beginning, what internal structure will there be, how many and which topics will be addressed in the first round? This is a whole field of questions that are at least in part important enough to be included in civil society decision-making. Now that I am writing this, I myself do not yet have a complete overview of this field. Perhaps you have similar experience and can help in advance?

One of the functionalities of the civil democratic platform will be that participating Open Actors can address the supporters they currently have access to and ask them to support them on the platform. And on the other hand, it will also mean that voters who know and find a civil society actor trustworthy who does not yet participate will be able to ask him to also participate as an Open Actor in the civil democratic system. In this way, participation in the civil-democratic project will grow soon.

Another important part of the realization will be further research. The social and political sciences have for such a long time been preoccupied solely with the existing institutions of partitioning representation that Civil democracy is

far from having answered all questions. The number of related research questions is large↑, so if you as a researcher or
in a position to organise and enable research have the opportunity to support this research, use it!

Step 6: Accompany the work of civil democracy
Now the GSC and with it global civil democracy begins to
work. GSC members will find a way of cooperation and a
form how they can behave and be perceived externally as the
voice of the world population and global civil society. They
will find a working rhythm in which they present upcoming
decisions to the world's population and global civil society,
and will thus regularly draw the attention of global media to
how many people in the civil democratic model participate
in these decisions and what they decide together.

In this stage it is important to stick to the project – the
idea of the representative democratic part of civil democracy,
and thus the basis of its stability, is that the semi-interested
people are also involved through their representation in civil
society. But in contrast to representative democracy, the special advantage, apart from actor openness, is the possibility
of participating responsibly in decisions of interest. The
more people actually participate responsibly in decisions and
thus show their willingness to bear the costs associated with
a decision that they consider to be good in their daily lives,
the greater the persuasiveness of the civil-democratic project.

Direct participation in civil democratic decisions also in-
creases the contribution to saving the world. Saving the
world will not be possible if we are not prepared to change
our individual behaviour in important areas. Once the work
of civil democracy has begun, make it a habit to see what
decisions are pending, what your Open Actors think about

it, what arguments there are and what you think of these arguments, and use the opportunity for direct democratic co-decision making.

Step 7: Accompany political implementation

The GSC is formed bottom-up. Unlike, for example, the UN General Assembly, which was created by decision of the signatory nations of the UN Charter and had certain powers from the outset, it starts out without any real decision-making power. But it is anything but unimportant. The efficiency of civil democracy lies in the fact that decision-making processes can take place quickly, involving a very large number of people in a responsible manner. Within a short time, the official bodies of the United Nations will come under great pressure to justify their decisions if they do not take into account the position of the world population represented by the GSC and a possible civil democratic process.

Triggered by the example of the GSC, civil democratic applications will also emerge in other contexts, as discussed in Chapter 8 above.

- If municipalities use the civil-democratic model for upcoming major decisions, they can involve all civil society actors and the citizens themselves and thus achieve greater legitimacy and acceptance of even problematic decisions.
- If European civil society uses the civil-democratic model to find perspectives for the further development of the EU that do not fall victim to the much-lauded democratic deficit, this is a great opportunity for the legitimacy and cohesion of the continent.
- If non-European societies use the civil-democratic model in order to involve their now so much better educated population and above all their young people in decisions affecting society as a whole on a sustainable

121

basis, this is a great opportunity to fight corruption at its roots and restore people's responsibility for their own lives.

- If US civil society uses the civil-democratic model to develop solutions for certain policy areas that can be accepted by the moderate forces on both sides, despite the strong polarization of the political public, this is a great opportunity for the US to find its way out of the long-lasting blockade in which it currently finds itself.

Of course, all these processes will not just happen by themselves. They need people who can push them forward and convince the relevant actors that it makes sense to follow this path. It would be great if you could be involved in your own environment to ensure that wherever democratic procedures today are unsatisfactory or perhaps even non-existent, the opportunity for the application of civil democracy is seized.

And it would also be great if you didn't just stay with the civil democracy project as long as it's a promising idea or an electrifying project. But also in the more difficult phases that are guaranteed to come: when hackers try to undermine it, when the whole approach is normatively under attack, or when decisions are pending that personally demand that you change something in your life.

These difficulties will come. With your help, we shall overcome them. Saving the world is worth it.

Notes

Ch. 1 Saving the world

Pg. 3 "half of the world's higher life forms will be extinct": Wilson 2002.

Ch. 3 Beginnings

Pg. 15 "goals are followed": Deci und Ryan 2000. The theory of motivation applied here is described in more detail in the motivation chapters of Scholtz 2020a and Scholtz 2020b.

Pg. 15 „homeostasis": Strombach et al. 2016.

Pg. 16 „goals": DeShon und Gillespie 2005.

Pg. 16 "projects": Flusser 1994.

Pg. 15 "generate anticipation": Salimpoor et al. 2015.

Ch. 4 Europe

Pg. 30 "prohibition of marriages between relatives": Schulz et al. 2019.

Ch. 5 The long 20th century

A detailed version of the relations described in chapter 5 can be found in Scholtz 2016.

Pg. 38 evidence for parallel problems: For populism see Applebaum 2016; Formisano 2016; Arnold 2017; Rosenbaum 2017; Albright und Woodward 2018; for globalization see Chase-Dunn, Kawano und Brewer 2000; for terrorism Gelvin 2008; Jensen 2009; for economic crises Reinhart und Rogoff 2009; for increasing inequality Alderson und Nielsen 2002.

Pg. 41 damaged reputation of modernization theory: Knöbl 2003

Pg. 44 "large bureaucratic organization": Friedrich 1952; Merton et al. 1952; Hall 1963

Pg. 45 "revolution": Lees 1982; Lipold und Isaac 2009.

Pg. 46 "rise of secondary schooling": Flora et al. 1983; Goldin 1998; Rangazas 2002.

Pg. 46 "concept of the nation state": Wimmer und Feinstein 2010.

Pg. 47 ""iron law of oligarchy": Michels [1925] 2002.

Pg. 49 "norm of insight into historical guilt": Schefczyk 2012.

Pg. 51 missng institutions and inequality: Snower 1999.

Ch. 6 Problems of partitioning representation

Pg. 58 " clients of the workers' parties": Rueda 2005.

Pg. 58 "environmental issues in international negotiations": Phelan, Henderson-Sellers und Taplin 2013.

Ch. 7 Civil democracy

Pg. 66 "founding fathers": "the ultimate authority, wherever the derivative may be found, resides in the people alone" Madison [1788] 2012, p. 65; "Alle Macht geht vom Volke aus." GG Abs. 2.

Pg. 68 Pia Mancini: https://www.ted.com/talks/pia_m ancini_how_to_upgrade_democrac y_for_the_internet_era, or search for Pia Mancini on youtube.com.

Pg. 70 "irresponsible protest": Dyck 2009; Dyck 2010.

Pg. 70 "direct democracy": Frey 1994; Matsusaka 1995; Matsusaka 2005.

Ch. 8 Application variety and strategy

Pg. 87 "current level of dissatisfaction": z.B. Rothkopf 2017.

Pg. 93 FIFA: Becker 2013; Bean 2016.

Ch. 8 The adolescence of the world

Pg. 100 "Blame the politicians": Mann 1999, S. 19.

Pg. 100 Evil as universal attribute: e.g. Kant [1793] 2011, Teilhard de Chardin 1959.

Pg. 101 "efficiency of bureaucratic mass murder": Bauman 1998.

Pg. 101 "hate propaganda on the radio": Thompson 2007.

Pg. 101 ""Dialectic of Enlightenment": Horkheimer und Adorno 2001.

Pg. 101 Kuper: Kuper 1982.

Pg. 101 Mann, History of power: Mann 1986-2013.

Pg. 101 Mann, danger of democracy: Mann 1999; Mann 2005

Pg. 102 "value change": Inglehart 1977; Inglehart 1990.

Pg. 103 ""authoritarian personalities": Adorno 1964.

Pg. 103 "fascist movements throughout Europe": After early attempts that could easily be perceived as relativizing responsibility (Nolte 1963), the study of fascism as a pan-European phenomenon has established itself as quite a matter of course, see e.g. Schaller et al. 2004, Orlow 2009, Riley 2010, Pinto 2014, Bauerkämper 2017.

Pg. 103 „organic solidarity": Durkheim [1893] 1988.

Pg. 104 Snyder 2000, Mansfield und Snyder 2005.

P. 105 „"Who are these belligerent democratizers":Narang und Nelson 2009.

Pg. 106 In the post-war years, Konrad Adenauer (1876-1967), Robert Schuman (1886-1963) and Alcide de Gasperi (1881-1954) shaped European Christian Democracy, in which Christianity began to accept open democratic processes.

Ch. 9 Our way

Pg. 113 our website: http://www.civil-democracy.org

Pg. 120 "number of related research questions": Scholtz 2019b

Pg. 117 "texts": etwa Scholtz 2017b; Scholtz 2017a; Scholtz 2017c; Scholtz 2018a; Scholtz 2018c; Scholtz 2018b; Scholtz 2019a, collected in *Civil democracy reader* (Scholtz 2019c).

References

Adorno, Theodor W. 1964. *The authoritarian personality*. New York, NY : Science Editions.

Albright, Madeleine Korbel, und William Woodward. 2018. *Fascism : a warning*. New York, NY: Harper.

Alderson, Arthur S., und François Nielsen. 2002. "Globalization and the Great U-Turn: Income Inequality Trends in 16 OECD Countries." *American Journal of Sociology* 107:1244-1299.

Applebaum, Anne. 2016. „Ähnlich wie in den 1930er-Jahren." *Tagesanzeiger* http://www.tagesanzeiger.ch/ausla nd/amerika/Aehnlich-wie-in-den-1930erJahren/story/27519272 26.12.2016.

Arnold, Jeremy. 2017. „A Fair Look: Is Trump Really a Fascist?" https://medium.com/thewholesto ry/a-fair-look-is-trump-really-a-fascist-8bf981d4a6b3 31.03.2017.

Bauerkämper, Arnd. 2017. Fascism without borders : transnational connections and cooperation between movements and regimes in Europe from 1918 to 1945: New York: New York : Berghahn.

Bauman, Zygmunt. 1998. *Modernity and the Holocaust*. Cambridge: Polity.

Bean, Bruce W. 2016. „An Interim Essay on FIFA's World Cup of Corruption: The Desperate Need for International Corporate Governance Standards at FIFA." *ILSA Journal of International & Comparative Law* 22: https://ssrn.com/abstract=271495 7 (11.5.2017).

Becker, Ryan J. 2013. „World cup 2026 now accepting bribes: a fundamental transformation of FIFA's world cup bid process." *The International Sports Law Journal* 13:132-147.

Chase-Dunn, Christopher, Yukio Kawano, und Benjamin D. Brewer. 2000. „Trade Globalization since 1795: Waves of Integration in the World-System." *American Sociological Review* 65:77-95.

Deci, E. L., und R. M. Ryan. 2000. „The „what" and „why" of goal pursuits: Human needs and the self-determination of behavior." *Psychological Inquiry* 11:227-268.

Deshon, R. P., und J. Z. Gillespie. 2005. „A motivated action theory account of goal orientation." *Journal of Applied Psychology* 90:1096-1127.

Durkheim, Emile. [1893] 1988. Über soziale Arbeitsteilung : Studie über die Organisation höherer Gesellschaften. Frankfurt am Main: Suhrkamp.

Dyck, J. J. 2009. „Initiated Distrust Direct Democracy and Trust in Government." *American Politics Research* 37:539-568.

—. 2010. „Political Distrust and Conservative Voting in Ballot Measure Elections." *Political Research Quarterly* 63:612-626.

Flora, Peter, Jens Alber, et al. (Hrsg.). 1983. *State, Economy, and Society in Western Europe, 1815-1975, Volume 1.* Frankfurt: Campus.

Flusser, Vilém. 1994. *Vom Subjekt zum Projekt : Menschwerdung.* Bensheim [etc.] : Bollmann.

Formisano, Ron. 2016. „The Populist Tsunami of the Second Gilded Age." *Forum (2194-6183)* 14:281-294.

Frey, Bruno S. 1994. „Direct Democracy - Politicoeconomic Lessons From Swiss Experience." *American Economic Review* 84:338-342.

Friedrich, Carl F. 1952. „Some Observations on Weber's Concept of Bureaucracy." S. 29-42 in *Reader in bureaucracy,* hg. Robert King Merton, Alisa P. Gray, et al. Glencoe: Free Press.

Gelvin, J. L. 2008. „Al-Qaeda and anarchism: A historian's reply to terrorology." *Terrorism and Political Violence* 20:563-581.

Goldin, Claudia. 1998. „America's graduation from high school: The evolution and spread of secondary schooling in the twentieth century." *Journal of Economic History* 58:345-374.

Hall, Richard H. 1963. „The Concept of Bureaucracy - an Empirical-Assessment." *American Journal of Sociology* 69:32-40.

Horkheimer, Max, und Theodor W. Adorno. 2001. *Dialectic of enlightenment.* New York: Continuum.

Inglehart, Ronald. 1977. The Silent Revolution: Changing Values and Political Style. Princeton: Princeton UP.

—. 1990. Culture Shift in Advanced Industrial Society. Princeton: Princeton UP.

Jensen, R. B. 2009. „The International Campaign Against Anarchist Terrorism, 1880-1930s." *Terrorism and Political Violence* 21:89-109.

Kant, Immanuel. [1793] 2011. *Die Religion innerhalb der Grenzen der blossen Vernunft.* Berlin: Akademie-Verlag.

Knöbl, Wolfgang. 2003. „Theories that won't pass away: The never ending story of modernization theory." S. 96-107 in *Handbook of Historical Sociology,* hg. Gerard Delanty und Engin F. Isin. London: Sage.

Kuper, Leo. 1982. *Genocide : its political use in the twentieth century.* New Haven : Yale University Press.

Lees, Lynn Hollen. 1982. „Strikes and the Urban Hierarchy in English Industrial Towns, 1842-1901." S. 52-72 in *Social Conflict and the Political Order in Modern Britain,* hg. James E. Cronin und Jonathan Schneer. London: Croom Helm.

Lipold, P. F., und L. W. Isaac. 2009. „Striking Deaths: Lethal Contestation and the „Exceptional" Character of the American Labor Movement, 1870-1970." *International Review of Social History* 54:167-205.

Madison, James. [1788] 2012. „Essay 46, January 29,1788." S. 65-73 in *The federalist papers*, hg. Richard R. Beeman. New York: Penguin Books.

Mann, Michael. 1986-2013. *The sources of social power*. Cambridge: Cambridge University Press.

—. 1999. „The dark side of democracy: the modern tradition of ethnic cleansing and political cleansing." *New Left Review*:18-46.

—. 2005. The Dark Side of Democracy: Explaining Ethnic Cleansing. Cambridge: Cambridge University Press.

Mansfield, Edward D., und Jack L. Snyder. 2005. *Electing to fight : why emerging democracies go to war*. Cambridge, Mass.: MIT Press.

Matsusaka, John G. 1995. „Fiscal effects of the voter initiative - Evidence from the last 30 years." *Journal of Political Economy* 103:587-623.

—. 2005. „Direct democracy works." *Journal of Economic Perspectives* 19:185-206.

Merton, Robert King, Alisa P. Gray, et al. (Hrsg.). 1952. *Reader in bureaucracy*. Glencoe: Free Press.

Michels, Robert. [1925] 2002. Political parties : a sociological study of the oligarchical tendencies of modern democracy. New Brunswick, NJ; London: Transaction Publishers.

Narang, Vipin, und Rebecca M. Nelson. 2009. „Who Are These Belligerent Democratizers? Reassessing the Impact of Democratization on War." *International Organization* 63:357-379.

Orlow, Dietrich. 2009. The lure of fascism in western Europe : German Nazis, Dutch and French fascists, 1933-1939: New York, N.Y. : Palgrave Macmillan.

Phelan, L., A. Henderson-Sellers, und R. Taplin. 2013. „The Political Economy of Addressing the Climate Crisis in the Earth System: Undermining Perverse Resilience." *New Political Economy* 18:198-226.

Pinto, António Costa. 2014. *Rethinking fascism and dictatorship in Europe*. Basingstoke : Palgrave Macmillan.

Rangazas, P. 2002. „The quantity and quality of schooling and US labor productivity growth (1870-2000)." *Review of Economic Dynamics* 5:932-964.

Reinhart, Carmen M., und Kenneth S. Rogoff. 2009. *This Time is Different: Eight Centuries of Financial Folly*. Princeton: Princeton University Press.

Riley, Dylan. 2010. The civic foundations of fascism in Europe : Italy, Spain, and Romania, 1870-1945: Baltimore : Johns Hopkins University Press.

Rosenbaum, Ron. 2017. „Against Normalization: The Lesson of the „Munich Post"." *Los Angeles Review of Books* https://lareviewofbooks.org/articl e/normalization-lesson-munich-post/:5.02.2017.

Rothkopf, David. 2017. „Is America a Failing State?" *Foreign Policy* 10.5.2017: https://foreignpolicy.com/2017/0 5/10/is-america-a-failing-state-trump-fires-comey-fbi/.

Rueda, D. 2005. „Insider-outsider politics in industrialized democracies: The challenge to social democratic parties." *American Political Science Review* 99:61-74.

Salimpoor, V. N., D. H. Zald, et al. 2015. „Predictions and the brain: how musical sounds become rewarding." *Trends in Cognitive Sciences* 19:86-91.

Schaller, Dominik, Rupen Boyadjian, et al. 2004. *Enteignet, Vertrieben, Ermordet. Beiträge zur Genozidforschung.* Zürich: Chronos.

Schefczyk, Michael. 2012. Verantwortung für historisches Unrecht: Eine philosophische Untersuchung. Berlin: de Gruyter.

Scholtz, Hanno. 2016. Two Steps to Modernity : What Crises, Terror, and Other Parallels Tell For Understanding the 20th and Shaping the 21st Century. Konstanz/Zürich: http://www.lulu.com/content/paperback-buch/two-steps-to-modernity/19042501.

—. 2017a. „Zweite Moderne erklären, Wandel erwarten. Die soziologische Erklärung der Zweistufigkeit der Moderne und ihre Konsequenzen." DOI: 10.13140/RG.2.2.20531.73762.

—. 2017b. „Can the internet improve politics." DOI: 10.13140/RG.2.2.25564.90249.

—. 2017c. „Idea, background, and conditions for the implementation of network-based collective decision-making." DOI: 10.13140/RG.2.2.31175.80803.

—. 2018a. „Weber's question, Burt's answer: A groups under roofs network model of Western specificity." DOI: 10.13140/RG.2.2.34703.84647/1.

—. 2018b. „Structure and math of Civil democracy."DOI: 10.13140/RG.2.2.15671.37286.

—. 2018c. „Civil democracy: How partition led into social crisis and what we need to fix it."DOI: 10.13140/RG.2.2.22083.25121.

—. 2019a. „Civil democracy, oder: Was Klimawandel, Migration und Populismus mit dem Christentum zu tun haben - und was wir tun können." *Wedecide working paper* 5.

—. 2019b. „Researching problems of partitioning representation: Starting a research network on understanding and overcoming the partition paradigm." S. 147-161 in *The Civil Democracy Reader*, hg. Zürich.

—. 2019c. *The Civil Democracy Reader*. http://bit.ly/Civil-democracy_Reader_190911.

—. 2020a. Mediensoziologie: Eine systematische Einführung. Wiesbaden: Springer.

—. 2020b. Soziologie: Eine systematische Einführung. Wiesbaden: Springer.

Schulz, Jonathan F., Duman Bahrami-Rad, et al. 2019. „The Church, intensive kinship, and global psychological variation." *Science* 366:eaau5141.

Snower, Dennis J. 1999. „Causes of Changing Earnings Inequality." hg. Bonn: Institute for the Study of Labor (IZA).

Snyder, Jack L. 2000. From Voting to Violence: Democratization and Nationalist Conflict. New York: W. W. Norton.

Strombach, T., S. Strang, et al. 2016.
    „Common and distinctive
    approaches to motivation in
    different disciplines." S. 3-23 in
    *Motivation: Theory, Neurobiology and
    Applications*, hg. B. Studer und S.
    Knecht. Amsterdam: Elsevier
    Science Bv.

Teilhard De Chardin, Pierre. 1959.
    Der Mensch im Kosmos. München :
    Beck.

Thompson, Allan (Hrsg.). 2007. *The
    Media and the Rwanda Genocide*.
    London: Pluto Press.

Wilson, Edward O. 2002. *The future of
    life*. London : Little Brown.

Wimmer, Andreas, und Yuval
    Feinstein. 2010. „The Rise of the
    Nation-State across the World,
    1816 to 2001." *American Sociological
    Review* 75:764-790.